EDINBURGH REVIEW 120

Causeway

Subscription Rates

Individual subscriptions (3 issues annually) £17 / $27 / €27
Institutional subscriptions (3 issues annually) £34 / $54 / €54

You can subscribe online at www.edinburghreview.org.uk or send a cheque to *Edinburgh Review* 22a Buccleuch Place, Edinburgh, EH8 9LN

Back Issues are available at £5.00 each.

Edinburgh Review is a partner magazine with eurozine www.eurozine.com

Edinburgh Review

EDITOR: Brian McCabe
ASSISTANT EDITOR & PRODUCTION: Jennie Renton
REVIEWS EDITOR: Michael Lister
WEBSITE DEVELOPMENT: Peter Likarish

ADDITIONAL ASSISTANCE FROM: Hannah Adcock, Julia Böll, Tim West and Ryan Van Winkle

Published by Edinburgh Review
22a Buccleuch Place
Edinburgh EH8 9LN

edinburgh.review@ed.ac.uk
www.edinburghreview.org.uk

ADVISORY BOARD:
Robert Alan Jamieson, Gavin Miller,
Colin Nicholson, Faith Pullin, Randall Stevenson

ISSN 0267 6672
Edinburgh Review 120 ISBN 978-0-9555745-0-4

© the contributors, 2007

Printed and bound in the UK
by The Cromwell Press Ltd,
Trowbridge, Wiltshire

Edinburgh Review
   is supported by

Contents

Editorial *Brian McCabe*	7
FICTION	
Trapped	9
Trapped Again *Bernard MacLaverty*	12
The Toilets at the End of the Hemisphere *Glenn Patterson*	38
Molly Fox *Deirdre Madden*	93
Ticking the Boxes *Ron Butlin*	101
POETRY	
Tom Paulin	22
Alan Gillis	35
Frank Ormsby	44
Fred Johnston	53
Leontia Flynn	62
Howard Wright	72
Medbh McGuckian	90
Sinéad Morrissey	92
Dawn Wood	99
Nick Laird	107
Kapka Kassabova	118

ARTICLES

A Terrible Beauty — 17
Bernard MacLaverty and the short story of the Troubles
Matthew McGuire

Weeds and Wild Flowers — 27
Eleanor Burnhill

On the Making of a Playwright — 55
Brian McAvera

Renaissance Fisherman — 64
Michael Faulkner

Stewart Parker's Scottish Play — 81
Marilynn Richtarik

Northern Ireland Troubles Archive — 110
Andrea Rea

Irish Stories? Filming the Troubles — 112
Eamonn Hughes

PHOTOGRAPHS

Lammas Fair Ballycastle — 47
Alastair McCook

Belfast in the Seventies — 75
John Gilbert

REVIEWS — 121

Editorial

In his article 'A Terrible Beauty', Matthew McGuire argues that 'Northern Irish poetry can be seen as fulfilling the Yeatsian promise: a "terrible beauty" born out of a bloody union between politics and violence.' From the evidence of the poetry we publish in this issue, that 'terrible beauty' has grown up into something both robust and sophisticated. Indeed, one of the main reasons for choosing to focus on Northern Ireland was the range and depth of Northern Irish poetry submitted to the magazine. Alan Gillis, who teaches English Literature and Creative Writing at the University of Edinburgh, reinforced my conviction by soliciting a further wealth of poems. I am very grateful to him for his advice and help, as I am to Bernard MacLaverty for his. Bernard's own work is featured here in the form of two delightfully comic 'Your Man' tales, while some of his more serious short stories are considered in depth in 'A Terrible Beauty'. We also have new fiction by Deirdre Madden and Glenn Patterson, articles on drama by Marilynn Richtarik and Brian McAvera, Eamonn Hughes on the cinema of the Troubles, Eleanor Burnhill on 'Troubles tourism' and a portrait of a 'Renaissance fisherman' by Michael Faulkner, who lives with his wife and dogs in a wooden cabin on the otherwise uninhabited island of Islandmore on Strangford Lough.

'Causeway' continues *Edinburgh Review*'s tradition of presenting creative and critical work of the highest quality by established and lesser known writers, and of celebrating Scottish culture but also looking beyond, to other countries and cultures. Next, we go to Poland…

Brian McCabe, Editor

Bernard MacLaverty

Trapped

Your man knew he should never accept hospitality. Always insist on a hotel. That way you can sit in the bar for as long as you like. But the Dublin crowd inviting him pleaded poverty and asked him to stay with one of their members. He would be met at the airport by a Mrs O'Neill and would stay at her place.

On the flight as he picked over the tiny snack the airline had provided he wondered about his hostess – perhaps a young and beautiful widow. She would be standing there, the blush never far from her cheek, with his name felt-tipped in black letters – YOUR MAN the card would say.

When he came out of Customs the woman holding his name was white haired and stooped – in her eighties. Your man felt such a rush of concern that he took her by the elbow and escorted her in the direction of the taxi rank but, sensing his intention, she indicated she had a car. Out of the corner of his eye your man noticed an even older man following them as they slowly traversed the concourse. The old woman paused and introduced him as her husband, Mr O'Neill. He had a red face and a white toothbrush moustache. Despite their Irish name they both spoke the poshest of public school English. They were dressed in a variety of interchangeable green tweeds.

After much to-ing and fro-ing in the dark car park they found the car and she offered your man the passenger seat. It was a two door model and she tilted the seat forward and with much clucking and manoeuvring began to angle her husband into the back. He slowly jack-knifed and trembled a little as he leaned his weight on her guiding forearm. He fell onto the bench seat and remained slumped at that angle. She claimed, as she walked around the car, that her husband's eyesight was not as good as it used to be. In the driver's seat she was not tall enough to see over the dashboard. Her nose tilted up to afford her a better view of the road and she tended to waggle the gear stick a lot. Your man was not afraid, just very, very tense. He didn't want to distract her by asking questions and yet didn't feel comfortable sitting in silence. He wanted to address the tilted husband but didn't know where to begin.

'We live around the corner from the venue,' said Mrs O'Neill. 'We used to have a place in the country. But it was too big – cost us a fortune. So we sold up and bought this little flat in the centre of town. We love it, don't we, dear?' She took her eyes off the road to slant the question over her shoulder into the back seat. Your man pressed down hard on the floor with both feet.

'Yes.' He cleared his throat and asked, 'Do you like Guinness?'

'Yes.'

'I used to be a director.'

'In movies?'

'No.'

'What then?'

'Of Guinness.' Your man looked back at him – he was still tilted – but now he was seriously rich and leaning to the right. 'I have a barrel at home. We can have some when we get back.' These people could pay his hotel bill for a year and not even notice.

The rain came on. The wipers purred and ticked, making everyone aware they were not talking.

By the time they turned into a city centre courtyard it was raining heavily. The old woman was animated by the rain and leapt from the car and opened the up-and-over garage door. She leapt back in again and drove the car inside. They traversed the courtyard to the multi-storey block of flats. In the lift the old woman said, 'We're on top. The fifteenth.'

At the door her husband went through a frenzy of pocket searching and muttering and key turning. There were three locks.

'Living here,' she said, 'you can't be too careful.'

Inside, the space seemed cramped because of too many sofas and chiffoniers and fringed lampshades and bureaus and ormolu clocks. It was crowded like an antique shop with no room to walk between the items. The bedroom had the same feel to it.

When your man joined them in the sitting room they were watching television.

'Forgive us,' she said. 'My husband is waiting on a programme. An examination of Dutch business methods. Would you like a Guinness?' Your man nodded almost too enthusiastically.

'A pint or a half pint?'

'I'm on my holidays – I'll go for the whole pint.'

'Good man.' She went out and came back immediately wearing her raincoat. She had a wicker basket on her arm. 'Darling, can I borrow your keys? I don't know where mine are.' She turned to your man. 'We keep the Guinness in the garage.'

Your man and Mr O'Neill sat without addressing each other for about the next twenty minutes. He snorted occasionally at things on the screen. Eventually above the noise of the television a key was heard to turn in the front door lock. The old woman shuffled in – balancing with great care her basketful of drink, smiling. The rain gleamed on her shoulders. She set the basket down and dealt out some olive green coasters onto the polished wood beside them – one for her husband and two for the guest. Then she handed your man, the D handle towards him, two half pints of Guinness in cute dimpled glasses.

'Not a drop spilled,' she said.

With a sinking heart your man just knew this was the end of the night's drinking, not the beginning. Even if she asked him he couldn't have another. At her age – three locks and fifteen floors and a courtyard full of puddles and an up-and-over garage door. And the same on the way back.

The programme on Dutch business methods droned on and the old man sat forward on his sofa, cupping his ear. He left his half pint untouched for the best part of half an hour. When the programme was over he decided to lock up. Both of them yawned loudly. Chains rattled and bolts clunked into place.

Mrs O'Neill asked if there was anything else she could get your man.

He said he'd had more than plenty to eat on the plane. As for her – she was completely jiggered and was going to bed. She carefully negotiated her way about the room unplugging things, including the television, and switching off standard lamps.

'My husband and I are early-bedders,' she said, 'but that should put no constraints on you.'

Your man decided to call it a day and went to his guest bedroom. He could hear the old ones talking distantly. He sat down on the bed, fully clothed and considered the fact that it was nine-thirty in one of the most vibrant cities in the world and he was triple locked into a chintz and ormolu bedroom fifteen floors up, hungry and without a drink.

Trapped Again

Your man had, for the last couple of days, been suffering from Sudden Bad Foot & Limping Syndrome. It was the gout or some other not-to-be-investigated matter. But he was determined, with the aid of a stick and your woman, to go to a BAFTA screening. When they got to the Odeon your woman went off to check them in. He knew the stairs would be a problem so he asked an Odeon girl if there was a lift. She saw the stick and understood. She took him to the first floor in the service elevator.

'What are you going to see?' said Odeon girl.

'*A Beautiful Mind.*'

'That's nice. It's BAFTA, isn't it?' She raised an eyebrow. 'That's on the ground floor tonight.' So she stepped out of the lift and pressed the button to send him to the ground floor again. On the journey down the lift gave a number of wheezes and shudders and there were some clanking noises like a village pump handle falling off and everything jerked to a halt. No matter which button your man pressed the lift would go neither up nor down. He eyed the alarm button. Scarlet red – dangerous looking. He tried to open the doors by shoving them back. Nothing.

Your man imagined pressing the alarm button and the effect it would have – people streaming out of every one of the ten cinema screens, maybe dozens trampled to death underfoot. They'd have to stand outside in the rain for the duration of the emergency, cursing whoever was responsible. Or was it like one of those teeth-grinding car alarms that go off in the middle of the night which go on for ages at great volume and drive everyone in the vicinity mad? More pressing of up and down buttons had no result. Five minutes. The movie would be starting. And if there was one thing your man hated it was going into a movie late. Even missing the credit sequence was annoying. Your woman would be wondering where the hell he was. Red for danger. Don't be alarmed. But what else could he do?

He took a deep breath and for the first time in his long life he pressed an alarm button. Tring! It was like a wee door bell. Tring. Is Jimmy in? And again. Tring. It didn't go on and on. Tring. A distant Odeon girl voice.

'Yes, we can hear you. Just a moment and we'll get you out. No need to keep pressing the alarm.' That's him told. So he waits. And waits.

Somewhere in your man's beautiful mind he remembers reading about the inventor of the elevator – the name Otis persists. The first one was in a five-storey china shop on Broadway and it was essential to Mr Otis's invention to have a safety device that when a steel cable broke the elevator didn't fall. He was glad to have read about it all those years ago. If it did fall he could always try the experiment of anticipating the impact and jumping into the air just prior to that moment.

Other male staff have been called in and their voices can be heard. They do not inspire confidence. 'Ohhh shit', 'I've never seen one like that', 'Is it this way or that?', 'We're going to have to turn the power off', 'Where's the bloody brake things?' They don't know your man can hear them. Then a change of voice and someone shouts, 'Is the customer okay?'

'Yes, the customer is fine.' As soon as he has shouted his reply it crosses his mind to mention his ailment. Should he say, 'Not altogether fine. I'm suffering from Sudden Onset Bad Foot & Limping Syndrome.' Something deep inside tells him that this is neither the time nor the place.

'We'll have you out of there in no time, sir.'

Your man takes the weight off his bad foot and leans against the wall and looks around him. On the floor are hundreds of cellophane wrapped rolls – for hot dogs – the kind of white bread you suck rather than chew. And four cardboard boxes marked 'one of four' and 'two of four' and so on up to four. One box is open and contains leaflets for the spring season at the Tron Theatre. A different voice shouts, 'We're going to wind you up to the first floor, sir'. Then the same voice drops into conversational mode. 'Which way is up?' There is a small squeaking noise over the next five or ten minutes. All hope of seeing *A Beautiful Mind* has gone. The Odeon girl is on the first floor. They are trying to line up the lift with the floor exactly so's the gates will open.

'Just give me another two inches,' she shouts.

'That's what the wife says all the time,' says one of the winchers. Your man sees light and the doors give a wobble and open a fraction. He puts a smile on his face to walk out with. But the door sticks. He sees wee pink girlie fingers trying to force the inner doors open.

'If I lose my fingers I'll sue,' she says. But it doesn't work. There's a confab on walkie-talkies. The decision is to open the bottom floor doors and wind the lift down. So they try that. Squeaky, squeak, click, squeakity, clickety.

'It's harder winding it down than bringing it up.' It all takes for ages. There is only so much pleasure a man can get out of a Tron Theatre brochure of future events. The print is so small and the lay-out so trendy that he would have to get his glasses out and he can't be bothered. He considers sucking a roll. Comfort food. It is not a realistic way to pass the time. Occasionally they shout encouragement.

'It'll not be long now, sir.'

'We'll have you out of there in a jiffy.' But that only makes it seem more serious. Like he's trapped down a mine or in a submarine. How many jiffys in half an hour? The lift doors are brown, the magnolia light-shade is of plastic and is broken. Somebody has scratched a name on the inside of the door. How or why did he do that? A lift which only journeyed to one floor. You wouldn't have time to get your penknife out, never mind carve *Jimbo* on it. Clickety, squeaky, squeak, click, squeaky. One of the winders' voices floats clearly down the shaft. 'This happened in Dundee,' he says. Your man can hear him panting. The way he says it, whatever he is doing must be hard work.

Eventually the lift reaches the bottom floor and still the inner doors won't open. The girlie fingers peep in again, four little pink pads. And again your man arranges a smile on his face for his exit. He tries to think of a good joke but nothing comes. He imagines the effect a good joke would have, but cannot imagine the joke itself. Odeon girl will turn to her mates and say, 'You'll never believe it. He was trapped in the lift for half an hour and when he came out all he said was dot, dot, dot… Isn't that hilarious?' But no joke comes and nothing happens. There is a great rattling of keys and grunting and little indecipherable swears as things fail to engage or go click. Now he hears his wife's voice clearly. She has given up on the movie and wants her husband rescued before she goes home.

'What about the Fire Brigade?' she says. When he was a child he called it the Firemigade. It has since become a sensible word in his house. By this time someone of the managerial class has arrived – someone who is addressed as Mister. Mister Eliot. He will take the decision to call the firemigade. Your man hears Odeon girl talking to his wife. Comforting her. She urges your woman to shout words of encouragement – which she does. The words come in through a little grille beside the light.

'They've sent for the Fire Brigade. Are you alright, love?' Your man and his wife had never been ones for Public Displays of Affection and the shouted word 'Love' is a source of some embarrassment.

'I'm fine,' shouts back your man. They can't hear him as well as he can hear them. He's fine but furious. Why does he keep trying to think of witty things to say when he gets out? Instead of 'I've drafted a letter to my solicitors on the back of this theatre brochure. Woe betide you and your cinema!', weak jokes about soft bread rolls or about his recently acquired encyclopedic knowledge of the Glasgow theatre season are uppermost. Away in the distance he hears the growing nee-naw, nee-naw of a firemigade. It gets louder and louder, then stops. Clumpy sounds, several new voices. Voices of authority.

'Are you all right in there ?' Basso profundo.

'Yes.' Tremolo.

The Fireman decides he wants the lift winched up again to the first floor. There is some muttered discussion and hesitation from the muscle team aloft.

'I'm in charge here – keep it going.' The Fireman seems very positive. Clickety, squeaky, squeak, click, squeaky, clickety, clickety, clickety.

'It's easier than winding it down.'

Your man feels no sense of movement. He has no idea whether he's going up or down. When he reaches the first floor the door is dragged open a half an inch by big black rubber-gloved fingers. But it won't open.

The Firemen talk. 'We don't want to have to dismantle it.'

'No way,' says somebody who sounds like Mister Eliot. Your man envisages cowering against the back wall trying not to look at the acetylene brightness and fizzing sparks bouncing around him as they cut their way in – in time for breakfast. Safe but with acetylene burns on the retina.

'Up a bit,' shouts the Fireman. Something somewhere is snagging or jamming.

'Down a bit.' There are a number of loud thumps and bangs. The doors open. Your man sees a Fireman's wellington boots. Navy uniforms rise to yellow helmets. There is a crowd. Your woman, cinema managers, usherettes selling ice cream, bystanders.

But the customer is between floors. All they can see of him is his head and shoulders. For him the ground is belt high. The Fireman offers your man a hand to pull him up.

'I've a bad leg,' says your man without wanting to go into the whole Unexplained Sudden Onset Bad Foot & Limping Syndrome. 'That's why I'm in the lift.'

'Can you get yourself up here?' The Fireman makes him turn his back on the assembled company and raise himself to sit on the threshold. Then he feels Fireman's hands slide under his oxters and he is pulled up the way a willick would be pulled from its shell. Your woman comes forward for a kiss. A Public Display of Affection. It's like the final scene of a Hollywood movie. The Odeon girl smiles warmly. After the kiss your man shrugs and grins. He can't think of anything witty in the circumstances. He shakes hands and backslaps the Fireman as they walk down the carpeted stairs.

Then the Fireman says, 'You wrote that book, that thing about… eh, about…'

'Yes, I did.'

'My girlfriend read it.'

Matthew McGuire

A Terrible Beauty
Bernard MacLaverty and the Short Story of the Troubles

A simple question – how does art respond to conflict? In the case of Northern Ireland poetry is generally believed to offer the most sustained and meaningful form of literary engagement with the lived reality of the Troubles. The North bucks current literary trends whereby it is the novelist that enjoys pseudo-celebrity status. And it is no longer just Heaney, if in fact it ever was. Longley, Muldoon, Carson and McGuckian are all distinct voices, headliners in their own right, not merely a supporting act. If the Troubles have been bad news for Northern Irish society, the same might not necessarily be said about its poetry. A more thoughtful view might point toward the raised stakes for art in lieu of the consummate failure of official narratives to make sense of the situation. Poetry is after all a special form of utterance, capable of articulating a kind of truth that remains obscured, elided and unsaid within other forms of discourse. Northern Irish poetry can be seen as fulfilling the Yeatsian promise, a 'terrible beauty' born out of a bloody union between politics and violence. In a Literary Olympics of the North, if such a thing could be imagined, poetry would undoubtedly win gold. Drama – Brian Friel, Stewart Parker, Christina Reid et al – would take silver, with prose, led by the 'Troubles trash' thriller, limping over the line in third place. Patricia Craig's introduction to the anthology of Ulster prose, *The Rattle of the North* (1992), is part caveat, part apology: '[I]t is well known that conditions in the North of Ireland, from Plantation times on, were never sufficiently settled to foster literary activity, and that the development of the novel, in particular, was consequently retarded.' If the novel is historically linked to narratives of national imagining, as Benedict Anderson argues, then we might not be surprised that it has failed to flourish within the volatile terrain of the North. However, if the Northern Irish novel is compromised there is another genre, one often overlooked, that can perhaps provide us with a fresh angle of approach. It is the short story. We might recall the Irish writer Frank O'Connor, himself a virtuoso of the form, who argued that the short story was most prevalent in societies confronted by instability, fracture and distemper. The famed Belfast Group of the 1960s suggests one point of coincidence in this particular map of Northern Irish writing. Whilst Heaney, Longley et al read poems to one another at their weekly writers' meetings, Philip Hobsbaum invited along a young laboratory technician from Queen's University who was writing stories in his spare time. It was, of course, Bernard MacLaverty.

More recently the short story has experienced something of a crisis of its own. Talk of its death abounds as publishers and book shops seem equally reluctant to get behind the genre. This has occurred alongside a growing lack of enthusiasm on the part of both mainstream and literary magazines to feature the short story in the way that they used to. The novel, of course, reigns supreme in the zeitgeist of the twenty-first century. Its fortune has risen under the aegis of the literary prize, the book group and the 'Buy One Get One Free' ethos of late capitalist consumer culture. However, it is this very feature of the short story, its brush against the grain of contemporary culture, where I wish to argue its residual value lies. If we may permit ourselves another imaginary leap, a court case to defend the genre, we might call on several key witnesses – Poe, Stevenson, Conrad, Chekov and Kafka to name but a few. In an Irish context the list appears equally distinguished – Moore, Joyce, O'Connor, Bowen. The historical and geographical spread of these writers suggests that rather than a mere appendage to the literary canon, there is something pervasive and fundamental about the form of the short story.

A flawed reading of the short story regards it as merely a composite part of the novel, a micro-narrative and by implication one that is derivative. As a consequence the short story becomes something trivial, throwaway and disposable. So how might we begin to rediscover the short story as a vital literary form? And how can it help us to approach the fraught subject matter of the Troubles? In *The Short Story: The Reality of Artifice* (2002), critic Charles E. May offers one useful point of departure:

> Although there is some justification for the common claim that the short story as a distinct literary genre began in the nineteenth century, the wellsprings of the form are as old as the primitive realm of myth. Studies in anthropology suggest that brief episodic narratives, which constitute the basis of the short story, are primary, preceding later epic forms, which constitute the basis of the novel.

Far from being secondary, the short story is more accurately seen as a primary form of narrative. It is a narrative distillation. It speaks of something fundamental, reminding us that as human beings we are essentially story-telling animals. With its condensation and tendency to focus on a single event, the short story bears remarkable likeness to our own everyday forms of communication. It is characterised by a certain sense of immediacy, a certain democratic tone if you will. It is its elliptical nature that makes the short story fundamental to any understanding of the lived reality of the Northern Irish Troubles. The criticism that short story offers only a truncated, unsatisfactory version of events is crucial. Consider this alongside the difficulty of explaining to the uninitiated much of what has passed for normal everyday existence in Northern Ireland since 1969.

Since 1977 Bernard MacLaverty has published five collections of short stories along with four novels. His stories eschew the familiar terrain of the thriller, with its focus on paramilitaries and security forces, and instead focus on the lives of ordinary people and their normal existence within the North. The title story from his 1994 collection *Walking the Dog* examines the fragile nature of everyday experience during the Troubles. A man walking his dog one evening is suddenly abducted by two men at gunpoint. They claim to be from the IRA and proceed to interrogate him in the back of a car, wanting to know if he is a Protestant and threatening to kill him. When the man says he doesn't believe in any of that stuff, the gunmen turn to the secret codes of sectarian identity politics – his name, where he works – in order to determine his religion. When this doesn't clarify the issue they ask him what he thinks of the IRA. In a moment of bravery the man declares, 'I hate you for doing this to me.' The gunman retorts, 'Spoken like a man… he's no more of a Fenian than I am.' The gunmen were actually Loyalists and had been attempting to trick the man into admitting he was a Catholic. They release him, telling him, 'No hard feelings,' and he is once again standing with his dog, back on a familiar Belfast street. The story reveals the sectarian identity politics that are a ubiquitous feature of Northern Irish life. It portrays the very real danger of finding oneself in the wrong situation, on the wrong side of this equation. However, it is the very mundane nature of the story that is most profoundly disturbing. In Northern Ireland the most normal activity can suddenly and terrifyingly be interrupted. Then, just as quickly, normality can resume. This pattern is familiar to many who experienced the violence of the Troubles first hand. Bomb blasts and gun shots are seldom anticipated. They are a shock, a jolt from the more familiar narratives of daily existence. The economy of the short story is crucial to achieving this effect. The anecdotal nature of the short story identified above is key here. It conveys what became a normal experience for people living in Northern Ireland, to suddenly have their lives interrupted by violence, fear and terror. The man's refusal to partake in the identity politics of the gunmen becomes a symbol for the everyday heroism of those who endured the Troubles. Just continuing with one's daily life – going for a walk, going to the pub – could become a gesture of quiet defiance.

Heaney famously referred to the sectarian loyalties of the North as a set of 'anachronistic passions'. The phrase implied a culture that had somehow been left behind by history. The North had fallen from the path of progress and become trapped in a cycle of distrust and mutual destruction. This narrative is captured in Bernard MacLaverty's story 'On the Roundabout' from *Matters of Life and Death* (2006). It begins with the most quotidian image – a husband, wife and two small children driving back into Belfast. Told from the perspective of the husband, the story has a casual colloquial tone. As the family nears the roundabout at the end of the motorway they see a hitchhiker being set upon by a gang of UDA men. In a powerfully disturbing turn of phrase someone produces a hammer and 'whacks the guy hitching in the face with it'. Seized by panic and anger, the father mounts the kerb and drives at the men. He bundles the hitchhiker into the car as the men stand back laughing. In the back of the car, the hitcher falls in and out of consciousness. There is black blood in his mouth and a hole the size of a ten pence piece at his temple. The father speeds round the roundabout to the nearby hospital. Again the story takes the most normal day and watches it all of a sudden become a horror scene. MacLaverty's concise and candid prose gives these moments their nauseating intensity. At the hospital the father attempts to give his name but the doctors and nurses don't want to know; neither does a nearby British soldier. The thought of facing the UDA across the witness box cools the father's rage: 'We know your registration, we know your whole family.' A few weeks later, a letter appears in the newspaper from the hitchhiker thanking the 'Good Samaritan' who had helped him that night. The narrative ends: '…wasn't that good of him? To tell the story.'

'On the Roundabout' becomes a symbol for a sense of metaphysical entrapment, the perpetual cycle of violence that defined the North during the Troubles. At the hospital this kind of violence has become so commonplace that there is no place for the detail of individual narratives. The Troubles have become a one-word phrase that elides individuals and their specific experiences of violence. 'On the Roundabout' is a story about stories. The moral significance of simply telling these individual stories is asserted. To merely say 'this happened' is fundamentally important and becomes itself a response to the violence. Perhaps this helps to explain why one of the most popular texts to emerge out of the Troubles is a book called *Lost Lives* (1999), comprising the individual stories of the 3,600 men, women and children who lost their lives during the Troubles. Eschewing the usual politicking it seeks to provide a record, a testimony of sorts, to the victims of the conflict. In a similar fashion, Bernard MacLaverty's work is a crucial part of the artistic response to the violence in Northern Ireland and as such demands further and extended scrutiny. When asked about what things were like living through the Troubles, the poet Ciaran Carson replied, 'I've lived in Belfast all my life and I still couldn't tell you a fraction of what's going on. All I can do is tell you stories.'[1] To fully comprehend events of the past forty years in Northern Ireland might be a feat beyond the imagining of any individual. Irregardless, a crucial part of any attempt to deepen our understanding remains the practice of simply telling stories.

1. Ciaran Carson interviewed by Rand Brandes, *Irish Review* No. 8, 1990.

Tom Paulin

Go You On Ahead – The Door's Open

No alert no moon the night thicklagged
thicklagged and safe –
– safe as houses or a homey cave –
indoors he hears some tune light
and ditsy on the wireless
like a code or a danger signal he wants to turn off
as he heads to the blackedout room below
what she calls her studio
– she stood in the kitchen cutting the crusts
from a fattish pile of white sandwiches
he can see the downturn of her wrist
as she pushes and the dry crusts they peel back
like bark or something else
and a phrase *trancher la question* slips into her head
and she hopes that no one in the merry crowd
just back from the pub
will guess their secret – still wet still new –
how keeping back from the others they took a quick turn
into the pitchdark woodyard its huge

strange resiny stacked dryness
just a few yards from her door
– us fighting men you know
it's for you lasses that we burn
now you won't deny me entry?
as he cupped her frizzy cunt in one hand
and stroked her bangs with the other
then kissed her on the lips really quite gently
like a thoughtful lover
I guess I've no choice she scoffed
as with her hand's help he put the hard nub
of his cock right up inside her
starting – stiff and certain in his forces' rubber –
starting really to ride her
as she stood rigid like a sentry
against a stack of timber
and swayed to his music
or stood he thought like a wooden stooge
for a stretched minute's tingaling
till – flibbertigibbet – he came and groaned
then gave a shrug
and ditched the slimy thing
like a lifebelt or a tiny dinghy
– now with her hand on the knifehaft
like a wooden tiller
and the last crusts peeling back like her cotton drawers
she feels quite sure of his shaft
till some guy in the next crammed noisy room
he echoes back to she can guess who in the smoke and fug
you were on the nightshift!

Convoy to Archangel

At the edge of the ice
we kept a rendezvous with two
big Soviet icebreakers
but little ice was left and that
was broken up
so I stood in the bows
in a damp pearly mist
that had suddenly come upon the ships
– I stood and listened
to the engine's thrust
interrupted by a swish and crunch
as the bows met a slab of ice
bobbing on the freed tide
then the long painful grind
as the slab rocked and brushed along the sides
the grince of the dissonance spoke to me
like the hinges of a heavy metal gate
designed in darkness
but working in daylight
in the permanent the classic daylight
that seemed – what it wasn't –
an experiment like this republic
as merchantmen swung at anchor
all through the summer of '43
waiting for a convoy escort that didn't come
there were growing queues of syphilitic seamen
outside a sickbay opposite the Dynamo

– summer nights of never setting suns
seamen semen syphilis those white
tainted nights I woke in like the young Stephen
imagining those pussy chancres
her pilgrim soul and – I don't know why –
the greenyblack word *encre*
but the words I put down were too hard
hard like rivets Soviet rivets
in Archangel Arkhangelsk old Russia
long grass and carved wooden houses settling
at odd angles – I see Lyuba now
laughing and magnificent
a can of sugared beer in one hand
a raw fish in the other
wooden clock like a Dutch clock above her head
while outside their cabin window
the river – it looks bankless – throws
back its dazzle like that thawing sea
– how could we be happy
in the darkest year of the war?
but happy we were as if Lyuba's brother
had painted us on a wooden panel
smiling and holding hands as we flew
high over Archangel like bride and groom
way beyond the mountain and the gloomy wood
– gloomy but purple like a seacliff
and we were the bridge above – the chattering
rainbow the watergaw aye the wind dog

at peace in something understood full stop
out of Yorkshire but of it still
thrawn and eloquent as ever I
who used to sing seashanties in the Yeats Room
who found after that calamitous convoy
– wooly smokebursts splitting ships yes the battle's din
found the one stable terrain that Arctic one
roof of the world whose rungs we hung on
– I still near the end of my life hear
the ice grinding on the steel plates the rivets
as I dip my pen and rub its tip on the bottle's rim
– rub it till it squeaks like a wet mouse

Eleanor Burnhill

Weeds and Wild Flowers
Political tourism in west Belfast

> *And there are other, less highly organised individuals, storytellers, musicians, dancers, 'local characters' etc, who are occasionally called upon to give performances. All such people act effectively as curators or custodians of the culture on behalf of the wider ethnic group.*[1]

As those studying tourism marketing note, most research shows fear and insecurity are major barriers to travel.

For years Northern Ireland, and its capital Belfast, was a tourism wilderness filled with 'anxiety and journalists' but, like weeds and wild flowers growing out of cracks in a pavement, a tentative tourism industry that recognised the 'curiosity' factor of the Troubles began to grow in the early 1990s. Much of this was led by local community groups in areas most affected by the conflict. Perhaps uniquely in a European city, taxi drivers adapted their businesses to take tourists on political tours.

Nowadays, however, a much wider tourism industry in Belfast is thriving, despite years of underfunding, and visitor numbers have returned to a level not experienced since the late 1960s. Ten years after the signing of the 1998 Good Friday Agreement, which signalled a period of tentative peace for

Northern Ireland, and in the two months before the March 7th elections for a new Legislative Assembly, I interviewed representatives from each of the four main political parties: the Democratic Unionist Party (DUP) and the Ulster Unionist Party (UUP), who traditionally represent unionists, and the main nationalist parties Sinn Fein and the Social Democratic and Labour Party (SDLP). I also interviewed those involved in community tourism and taxi drivers themselves, to find out what role they thought political tourism should have into the future.

Most agreed that the Troubles do have a role in Belfast's tourism product, but unsurprisingly for a state so divided by political tensions, there are divergent opinions about how this should be presented and marketed as a draw for visitors. The DUP's Diane Dodds, the first unionist to represent west Belfast, where many political tours take place, is keen to emphasise that these tours are just a miniscule part of the city's tourism and sees the way ahead in development such as the Titanic Quarter. Lord Mayor of the city and SDLP councillor Pat McCarthy expresses the concern that so-called 'terror tours' concentrate tourism in the hands of the very people who spent a lifetime destroying the city he loves, while Councillor Paul Maskey from Sinn Fein sees political tourism as a way to bring much needed employment to areas that suffered greatly during the Troubles and thinks taxi drivers struggle to give a balanced view to tourists. Meanwhile Bob Stoker from the UUP believes taxi drivers are uniquely placed to give political tours, which he thinks promote understanding of the conflict and could form part of the city's healing process – in their study of 'Dark Tourism', Lennon and Foley argue that tourist interest in disaster and atrocity is a growing phenomenon dating from the late 20th century, a kind of pilgrimage or way of memorialising death.

According to figures from the Belfast Visitor and Convention Bureau, in 2006 Belfast hosted 6.4 million visitors, with a turnover of £285 million to the economy of the city. In the same year, in Northern Ireland as a whole, 66 per cent of visitors were from Britain, which was bombarded during the thirty-year period of the Troubles with media images of the conflict. In his study of Northern Ireland's tourism image since the Troubles, David Wilson argues that whilst these images initially deterred visitors, particularly to inner city trouble spots, a 'curiosity' factor eventually began to creep in. Figures for 1986–87 show tourist numbers began to increase despite a rise in the level of violence and the fact that horrific incidents such as the Milltown Massacre of 1988 took place right in front of the television cameras.

This increase was recognised in the 1992 corporate plan of the Northern Ireland Tourist Board (NITB): 'Many people around the world have heard of Northern Ireland but often for the wrong reasons. They may be motivated to visit simply to see why there should be such a conflict in a modern society. The opportunity to harness this curiosity factor should not be overlooked…' This statement was described as 'disgusting beyond words' by the then Ulster Unionist MP Ken Maginnis, who said NITB was cynical to suggest that 'the suffering of the people of Northern Ireland can be packaged as a tourist attraction'.

A consultation document on Cultural Tourism for the NITB in 2006 demonstrates even greater confidence in harnessing this curiosity:

> It could be argued forcefully that heritage is the compelling proposition for a visit to Northern Ireland – our recent 'troubles' and the historical and community context from which they arose would play to the general perspective and still allow the visitor to take in castles and houses. However, this presents issues for the rest of the community not engaged in tourism and trying to come to terms with the 'hurt' and it probably has a limited shelf life.

Like ex-combatants and ex-prisoners, some of whom have been employed in community work and tourism since their release under the Good Friday Agreement, many taxi drivers now conducting political tours can lay claim to a personal role as storytellers of the conflict. Some taxi drivers were specifically targeted as victims during the Troubles, the first being Catholic Edward Campbell, who was found shot dead at a quarry on the Upper Crumlin Road in Belfast in 1987. Many others have since died in tit for tat killings, for their political affiliations or simply because they were easy targets.

Pat, who declines to give me his surname, but whose leaflet is among the taxi tour information at the Belfast Welcome Centre, is aware of this: 'The best training, I suppose, is to have been there and earned the T-shirt as the saying goes… I've always lived in Belfast and I've grown up through the Troubles.'

Taking me on a tour of the murals of west Belfast, which vividly depict the past and present of both loyalist and republican communities, he says:

'I suppose at a certain period there may have been a problem for either a Catholic driver going into the Shankill or a Protestant driver getting into the Falls, but taxi drivers were always in the firing line anyway... It was always easy to basically go down the phone book, pick out a taxi company, see what area it was based in and [be] pretty sure that you were going to have a Protestant or a Catholic driver and quite a few drivers paid the ultimate price for that.'

Another taxi driver, Billy Scott, who is a Blue Badge Guide, sees the tours as a natural evolution from shuttling journalists around the city during the Troubles – up until 1998, Belfast was a tourist wilderness: 'A lot of journalists would be here and they'd come along and they'd jump into a taxi and they'd say take me down to Drumcree or something – there's trouble down there... he'd be filing his report to the *Tokyo Times* and he'd be saying "informed source in Belfast has explained to me," and maybe that's a taxi driver... Since they signed the peace agreement it's becoming more and more popular: it probably started off with the likes of the backpackers. We used to get a lot of conflict resolutionists in the early days who would come and spread peace dust about the place... but this year alone there's twenty-six or twenty-seven cruise liners called into Belfast.'

People are often offered a tour as soon as they are picked up at the airport or ferry, and Scott points out the advantage that a cab provides an enclosed and comfortable environment where passengers can ask questions they might be afraid to ask on bus tours without knowing the political persuasions of the other passengers; and of course, taxi drivers 'will certainly tell you a story, so they will...'

In 1994, Citybus began operating a tour around some of the sights of west Belfast, entitled 'Belfast, A Living History'. The current Belfast 'hop on hop off' City Sightseeing bus takes in the wall murals of the Falls and the Shankill as part of a wider tour, but Scott says, 'The bus tours only go around the main arterial routes so they do, and they don't go into areas. In the taxi tours we encourage people to... ask us questions, so it's more sort of personal.'

Paradoxically, whilst the taxi environment may make it easier for visitors to relax and ask questions, there is little that tourism agencies can do to control and monitor the answers.

Tourism is now a major moneyspinner for Belfast and in order to protect this precious source of income, politicians from all the major parties are keenly aware that the industry has to be regulated to provide a quality product.

The Fifth Report of the Independent Monitoring Commission noted as recently as April 2005 that taxi firms were among a number of legitimate businesses being used by paramilitaries to move significant amounts of cash outside 'normal accounts'. While the taxi drivers themselves may not be members of paramilitary organisation, 'they may find themselves obliged to undertake tasks… such as the delivery of drugs or illicit tobacco'.

Taxi drivers are a wide and diverse group and there is no suggestion in the IMC report that the drivers involved in this kind of activity are the same ones conducting political tours, but clearly they could be.

There are many anomalies in the Belfast tourism product, but to iron out all of its idiosyncrasies, especially when it comes to presenting a topic as divisive as the Troubles, would take some of the personality and truth out of the experience. In future generations, taxi drivers will no longer have direct knowledge and will have to rely on history books or handed down stories and tour scripts.

Discussions are currently underway about setting up a museum of the Troubles but the NITB's consultation paper on cultural tourism notes:

> Furthering the idea is, of course, fraught with political and moral sensitivities and in order to be successful, will need to 'buy in' across the community. Both the Maze and Crumlin Road jail sites have been mooted as possible locations for such a museum while others are keen to see it established in a new building, which is devoid of political associations.

For communities in west Belfast, to be branded 'Living History' is both a blessing and a curse. Diane Dodds, who chairs Belfast City Council's Tourism and Promotion of Belfast sub committee, says that 'monkey in the cage' tourism can created a false impression that certain areas are dangerous. However, the drivers I interviewed say they are happy to drop tourists off anywhere they want to go, whether to have a cup of tea, buy a souvenir or walk around.

Across the peace line, on the Falls Road, Sinn Fein's Paul Maskey says his community is working to encourage tourists to do exactly those things: 'We would see political tourism as a massive draw to bring people into other parts of the city… the ones which have suffered the most throughout the war years in Belfast.' He works closely with organisations like Coiste, which look after the needs of republican ex-prisoners released under the Good Friday Agreement, many of whom have struggled to get jobs post-release.

Caoimhín Mac Giolla Mhín of Coiste takes educational groups, and sometimes interested tourists, on political walking tours, explaining the history of the Troubles from a republican viewpoint. He believes ex-prisoners provide a more authentic and honest experience than a taxi driver can. In more recent times, at the infamous peace lines which divide west Belfast, the tours have been handed over to loyalist ex-prisoners, who give a different side to the story.

'There are some small difficulties around the fact that people driving the black cabs come into the Falls, don't know the history of the Falls, they're giving a very, very sort of biased viewpoint of their unionist history, for example… so our theory and our reason why we linked up with loyalists is that they would not attempt to tell republican history and republicans would not attempt to tell loyalist, unionist history.'

Noel Large, a former UVF man who served sixteen years of a life sentence at the Maze prison for four murders he committed as a loyalist gunman, takes tourists around his community.

'As soon as the people on the tours know that you're an ex-life sentence prisoner and you've spent that long and that you're now involved in peace building work, they perk up… if you get an ex-republican prisoner and then a loyalist ex-prisoner doing the tour, what you'll get is both sides but it again will be biased either one way or the other…'

He is a passionate painter of murals which continue for both communities to communicate and commemorate the past. He says ex-prisoners should not have a monopoly on tours about the Troubles and believes taxis drivers are well placed to conduct tours, as they can adapt their routes to reflect changes in the community.

'I have facilitated the painting of a mural on Lanarkway security gates, which is part of the peace wall between the republican Springfield and the loyalist Shankill Roads, and while young people were painting it there were actually taxi drivers coming up and bringing tourists who wanted to see a painting in progress. So, yes, I think in some ways the taxi drivers have helped to promote the art on the walls. But at the same time I think that needs organised properly too, because you could be a street cleaner one day and a taxi driver the next, and then you're gonna bring people along who don't know anything about the area, and then you're gonna explain about a mural that you mightn't know too much about yourself.'

There is general agreement among the people I interviewed that the wall murals, which have been painted in Northern Ireland for almost a century, should be preserved for posterity. Some have become more militant since then, but many now depict historical scenes encapsulating political arguments and some display messages of peace, such as one in a traditional unionist area that reads, 'Can it change? We believe'.

According to UUP councillor Bob Stoker, 'Murals actually show the social history of a place… I'm not saying we should be celebrating the violence and the murder but we certainly shouldn't forget it and we shouldn't dilute it. Any community that had murals in them, it's part of their culture, it's part of their ethos and the violence that was associated with it is part of that particular area and particular culture.'

Dodds says of the tradition, 'One of the things that people like me and my community get distraught about… is that murals in Protestant areas are meant to be sectarian whereas murals in nationalist areas are portrayed as being somehow part of the cause. The reality is if you go up to the top of the White Rock and you stand there… you will see pictures of twelve hunger strikers as you drive up the road, you will see pictures renouncing collusion and so on. Nationalists and republicans have used murals to dominate areas and to portray an anti-British and sectarian message in those areas, just as much as they have been used the other way round… So there is nobody who's whiter than white…' She points out that in areas like the Shankill, many murals now reflect significant historical events and 'less that purely, nakedly sectarian intimidating thing.'

Belfast's lord mayor Pat McCarthy is perhaps the most sceptical about political tourism: 'I think it's being fed by… paramilitary linked groups who have spent a lifetime trying to destroy this city and murdering people on both sides of the divide and I think it's just another money-making enterprise for them. When we embarked on our Peace Process, there was something like nine or ten peace walls in this city. At the last count there was twenty-odd, so maybe we're going in the wrong direction.'

He says, having come through thirty years of mayhem, the city now needs to heal: 'Do we all come from Belfast or do we break it down into little fiefdoms?... Belfast is one city, with one people.' However, Bob Stoker believes that telling the story of the troubles is part of the healing process: 'We need to tell that story and we can't do it if it's sanitised. People just wouldn't understand the complexities…'

According to Lonely Planet, Northern Ireland is one of the 'must see' places of 2007:

> Freed from the spectre of the gun by cease-fires and political agreement, it's abuzz with life: the cities are pulsating, the economy is thriving and the people, the lifeblood that courses through the country, are in good spirits. Go anywhere in Northern Ireland and you won't be short of someone to talk to.

Given the freelance nature of taxi driving, you might not get the most knowledgeable guide, but you will certainly be told a story; 'weeds and wild flowers' can be much more enthralling than manicured lawns.

1. Buckley, Anthony and Kenney, Mary. 'Cultural Heritage in an Oases of Calm: Divided Identities in a Museum in Ulster'. *Culture, Tourism and Development. The Case of Ireland*. Ed Ullrich Kockel. Liverpool University Press, 1994.

Alan Gillis

Chalk and Cheese

She says: 'If I'm the barley, you're the hoe.'
Ho-ho. But no, between us, I often wonder,
who's the spellbound nation, who's the Führer.
She says: 'If I'm the fresh lime in the punch-bowl
of our love, you're the bitter tang of angostura.'
And when I was dragged to a darkened corridor
and found myself turning into, to my horror,
a gingered pulp of tallow and skin-rot
with bone-splintered, vein-burst, after-death eyes
she said: 'Love, come away from the mirror.'

You'll Never Walk Alone

She's dead set against the dead hand
of Belfast's walls guarding jinkered
cul-de-sacs, siderows, bottled sloganlands,
and the multinational malls' slicker
demarcations, their Xanadu of brands
entwining mind and income. Yet these replicas
atone for the brouhaha'd blare of the zones
she walks among, the bricked-in vigil of her home,

where they axed and hacked bark-stripped trees
and razed grass clearings, piled varnish-caked
crates and oil-slick tyres to a fire and stoned
dark-skinned refugees, broke Bacardi-Breezer
empties off kerbstones, paint-bombed windows,
raised their spray cans to new tenements,
built-up cans and butts like battlements
outside her door, and dreamed of burning green,
white and orange to ribbons that would rave
and rip through the dawn's zit of orange.

She walks by Little Britain merchandise,
made in China, and waits like a leper
in the darkened corridor of a debt advice
counsel room, listening to gangsta rappers
rapping that days slip by like grains of rice,
so she should shake her booty; that she is tapered
by time; that she should shed another skin;
that some days trampoline, flipping you outside-in.

'Such was the day' – I later heard her say,
soused in gin or doused with fontal waters
fallen from the apple-sliced, orange-peeling sky,
her shadow flaked as she wrangled for just
words – 'such was the day, not when guerrillas
ate the protestors' livers before a village
crowd for opposing oil drills on TV;
nor when the bright lights flared over Baghdad's
orange, rose and *Tomb Raider* blue targets
trained by oil wells firing a welcome, or adieu;

nor when the dawn green ocean's heart attack
churned coastlines into troughs of corpse-stew;
when the earthquake turned tenements to smokestacks;
but the day I broke down and bawled myself blue
by my front door's graffiti, falling on the cracked,
coloured kerb with every bill overdue,
wishing the ground would gobble me whole, and
a neighbour asked if I needed a hand.'

Glenn Patterson

The Toilets at the End of the Hemisphere

This is not at all the kind of place I could ever have imagined ending my life in: forty houses, a hotel, two churches, a fish and chip shop and what might be the last public toilets before Antarctica. I was born on an island the same size but most of the world away, so I suppose it rates as some sort of coincidence that the person who walked out of the stall as I stood doing battle with the hand-drier the Tuesday of last week was a man who had once threatened to kill my brother. He didn't speak. He didn't so much as pretend to wash his hands. By the time I had managed to dry my own he was long gone.

Which reminds me, there is never any soap in the last public toilets before Antarctica. I would complain but there is no one to complain to, anywhere.

On the back of the door of the stall that the man who didn't wash his hands came out of, a message has been scraped into the paint. Meet me here at 3pm good time guaranteed. Skeletal letters, the bare bones of the desire of the last person to cottage there. A body could waste away waiting.

There is an overpowering smell of lilies, through the slatted window high up on the wall. Lilies and seaweed. The ocean begins twenty feet from the door of the toilets. Behind the building is the road at the side of which the lilies grow. You have never seen lilies like these. Scores of them, head height, pistils pointing.

Meet me here at 3pm good time guaranteed. This is not a joke.

A little way down the road, past the stand of lilies, is the fish and chip shop where for six dollars Australian they will reach out the back into the ocean for a fish to gut and fry while you wait. It is closer to conjury than cookery. A girl with braces on her teeth batters a striped trumpeter for a neighbour she hasn't seen for all of ten days.

You been away?

Sick.

That's too bad.

Yes.

The trumpeter sizzles, she shakes the basket. To her left stand tanks of crab and lobster and fish that might have been invented by Andy Warhol. Seawater, the South Atlantic, laps under the wooden slatted mat overlaid on the concrete floor. In the visitors' book a woman from Surrey in England has written that this girl could learn some manners. She is sixteen. She is not bored, not exactly. She looks like all sixteen-year-old girls working in chippies the world over. Only her hair smells of striped trumpeter, orange roughy, blue morwong. At home the television has two channels. The radio will not pick up FM.

Small, large, or extra large? she asks.

Large, the neighbour says and the girl allows a scoop of chips to slide into its paper pocket.

On the far side of the narrow peninsula from the toilets in the graveyard, which the girl passes twice a day every day, lies Lucy Blizzard, who died, a long time ago, aged twenty-four. Beloved by all, the tombstone says.

I envy Lucy Blizzard, even if I am a little afraid of her stillness, her never anymore-ness.

In another part of the graveyard, it is whispered, is the grave of a British army officer put to death for loving his Aboriginal manservant. Loving isn't the word the whisperers use. I have looked for the headstone without success. Time and the saltwater air have seen to it that the slate is wiped clean. Nobody can tell me why some names fade and some names look as fresh as he day they were cut, like Lucy Blizzard's. Nobody can tell me where the manservant was buried. If he was buried.

I could not tell you anymore what I am doing here spending my days wandering between graves, smoking cigarettes outside the public toilets, on the shingle shore of this island where rainforest and surf beaches and volcanoes and farmland are thrown together, like the off-cuts of continents.

The mobile library rolls around every Wednesday. I am allowed three books and I ration myself to reading in the mornings and between the evening hours of six and eight. From nine and for as long as I can afford, I drink beer in the town's only hotel, one side of whose bar is the town's only betting shop and satellite receiver. Races from Melbourne, Hong Kong, Dubai: horses and ponies and sulkies. I have seen camels racing, for God's sake, their child riders tied on to their mounts. Maybe there is a virtue in just two channels.

There are no doors to lock on the public toilets. I walk in late at night and relieve myself against the last piece of porcelain this side of the South Pole with the sound of the waves running to shore at my back.

I find myself wondering about whales and urine, about Lucy Blizzard and the executed army officer. I find myself wondering about home.

Sometimes a coach will arrive and park outside the toilets. The passengers disembark and go inside and when they come out, complaining there is no soap, get back on board and drive the short distance to the fish and chip shop.

I try to ensure that I am on hand for these visitors. Distraction for me, rather than guidance for them. A guide is not required. The butcher's shop is marked, Butcher, the souvenir shop, Souvenirs. The chairlift signpost is the only other signpost in town. The chairlift is what they come here for. The chairlift is what I came for. From the top, I was told, you can see halfway down the island: rainforest and volcanoes and beaches out of office workers' dreams. Halfway is perhaps an exaggeration. Still. You can see smaller islands, a day's boat journey away, even now. The soldiers and convicts who were the first European inhabitants spent two years on these islands before they were able to reach this part of Tasmania.

Lucy Blizzard died three years after the first settlement was raised. Who knows why she was here. Poor Lucy Blizzard.

Many of the names still legible on the headstones are the names I hear spoken every day in the town. But there are no Blizzards that I have heard. The girl in the fish and chip shop is called Lorna. A boy comes into the shop to see her one night when I am there. He wears a washed-out T-shirt. Guns'n'Roses. I have seen him on the jetty where I stroll occasionally to watch the trawlers come and go with their pop-art catches. He bids Lorna g'day. Lorna shakes the chip basket, a little more energetically than normal.

Small, large, or extra large? she asks me.

I start into my meal before I am anywhere near the house. I have finished two of my three books and it is only Saturday. I am going to the hotel early tonight. I look back down the road and in the lighted window of the fish and chip shop I see Lorna and the boy in the Guns'n'Roses T-shirt facing one another across the chrome countertop.

A long time ago I lost a bet with my sister about the forename of the man this island was named for. Abel was the correct answer: the Bible's first murder victim. Tasmania was scarcely more than an idea to me then and not a very pleasant one at that.

My sister left home at sixteen, twenty-six years ago. We had a postcard, maybe twenty-five years ago. A koala up a eucalyptus tree. Don't worry, my sister wrote, I'm doing fine. Letter to follow. My parents set the postcard behind the clock on the mantelpiece, but no letter ever followed.

My parents are dead. Their car went off the road in Donegal last autumn. Drink had been taken.

I put an appeal out in the Australian papers. I linked up by satellite to radio stations in Sydney and Perth. When the funeral was over and the last of the relatives had left, I got on the computer and booked myself an open ticket.

That was October. Now it is May and I am in Tasmania.

The man who once threatened to kill my brother was here on a World Bible College bus tour. I found this out some days after I had seen him leave the stall of unrequited lust. I was in the hotel. A guy I had seen once or twice before, half a nose, no thumb on his left hand, started up a conversation. It was my accent he said, yes. Same as several of the men on the bus tour.

My brother was killed by someone else in the end. It was the way of the world in which he moved. There was never any shortage of people willing to point a finger or to pull a trigger. My brother was not a good man. I don't know if my sister knows he is dead. It was a famous case for a week or two back home. My mother said my father never recovered. My father said my mother never did. There is so much shame where I come from. Shame and prison conversions.

In Melbourne I found a woman in the phone book with my sister's name.

I called at the address, above a Vietnamese restaurant. A boy answered, thirteen, fourteen, in a sleeveless rugby jersey. The woman with my sister's name was the boy's mother. She was at work. It was mid-evening. I didn't bother asking about his father.

Tell her, I said, tell her…

The boy wanted to close the door. Yes?

Tell her I'll call another time.

I waited in the restaurant below the flat. An elderly man entered, pieces of card, six by four, in one hand. The cards had the names of popular songs written on them in red biro and had been wound around many times with clear tape. If you paid the man a dollar he would sing you any two of the songs. I only had a five. He sang at my shoulder the entire time I was eating. Actually, he sang me eleven songs. I hadn't specified which I wanted. Random selection. Phil Collins, Matt Monro. The freebie was Eddie Cochran. 'Look up in the sky, way up to the north./ There are three new stars, brightly shining forth./ They're shining oh so bright, from heaven above./ Gee we're gonna miss you, everybody sends their love…'

As I was paying the bill, I saw two women turn into the doorway leading to the flats above the restaurant. One was too young and the other… Well, how could anybody be sure after twenty-six years? Beyond all reasonable doubt sure.

There was a brochure in the vestibule of my guesthouse with a picture on the front of this town and its chairlift. I was open to suggestion.

I will in time perhaps persuade myself it was no more than suggestion what befell me last night. Suggestion laced with strong drink. I had been in the hotel too long before I stopped in at the toilets. As I stood there, my head resting on the tiles, filled with the smell of lilies, I knew it was not just the hotel I had been too long in. It was the easiest thing in the world I was suddenly so tired of to walk out of the toilets, across the twenty feet of shingle shore and into the sea. A stretch of the legs, my father used to say – I said, aloud. The sea was still and as cold as clay. With every step I seemed to shrink a little more. I imagined somewhere inside me a single point of light. The light that entered my eyes the moment I was born. I was walking out and I was walking in towards that light. A step beyond that… nothing but black.

Then the sand went from under me and my head, without my willing it, pulled in the opposite direction, and where before there had been scarcely a ripple, I saw her rushing towards me her arms outstretched, her hair a wild froth. All those centuries of stillness unleashed. She gathered me into her pulling me under and for a moment then I was looking into the eyes of Lucy Blizzard. They went on forever. I opened my mouth.

Take me, I wanted to say, but I felt her fingers on my lips, closing them.

I felt, as she set me down on the shingle, beloved.

The hotel, the fish and chip shop, the graveyard, the toilets. Not the kind of place to end your life in, but to live in, for now…

There is another graffito on the back of the stall door. *Practise acts of random kindness*.

This morning, I bought a bar of soap and left it by the wash hand basin. *Simple*, the label says.

This afternoon I will walk to the graveyard with a lily for Lucy Blizzard.

Frank Ormsby

Washington's Headquarters
White Plains NY

View by appointment only. Beware ticks.
Something opaque and sidelined on Virginia Road,
a farmhouse without a farm, half turned away
since the Battle of White Plains. In two days
the Revolution located elsewhere, the house withdrew
into the husk of more than itself.
Around it, for two centuries, the spread and rise
of a suburban city. Virginia Road belongs
to Byram Concrete and Wallauer's Paint Supply
and Nunway Complete Kitchens. Something contained.
Something preserved and absent. A silent space
where blinds fall and settle, dust-covers brush the floor.
That little dark rodent caught in the act
of going to ground had its back to us from the start.
Too late, too late to fix a silhouette
you could put a name to. No echo to detect
in the empty car-park or under the locked door.
The present is a thicket of sound, the dust of industry
a fine web in the trees, an invisible drift
across parkways, the new towers of White Plains.
Whatever haunts the present as the past's
unfinished business, lives endless, as it must,
in the moment we own it, then, as it must, defers
to what the moment offers: the tiniest grey mote

from the cement-works, the whole arch of the sky,
where, just now, a small plane is crossing,
the waiting-for-no-one, ceaseless rush and roar
of cars on the Taconic. What dirt track, what stony lane
dissolves in the foundations? A nameless line
from an old battle-plan sunk in Virginia Road,
untraceable now but taking the weight of the day
in its fourth century. The house is swallowing light.
It sits like an ageing uncle. You half-wish it spared
the long, spectral twilight, the life-support
with dials tuned to 'history' and 'heritage'.
You want it to drift like memory, released at last
from the tug of its moorings, or think of it setting sail,
dawn after dawn, on its one maiden voyage.
You imagine the kitchen table commandeered
for the War of Independence. The big map is unfurled.
Four plain jugs and the General's arms pin it in place.
Those faces at the side-window must belong
to Ann and Elijah Miller. When their eyes meet yours,
briefly they have the look of prisoners
in their own dream-house, allowed to glimpse, just once,
the trespass of the future. This must be the day
that Washington moved on, the day the Miller place
became Washington's Headquarters. You too skirt the edge
of what you might feel, or sense you ought to feel.
Time now to back away. You back away
until it is time, deferring, to turn your back
on that charged silence. Without missing a beat,
the present forgives you what you almost missed
in your almost-absence. Reclaims you as one of its own.

Some Spring Moons, North Circular Road

First the embarrassing moon,
so like nothing on earth
I bend my head at midnight,
closing the gates
on our threadbare planet.

Then the moon that seems to command
definitive utterance,
a clarifying take
so pure and simple no-one can understand
it was not obvious.

Next the dizzying moon,
and the moon that has no time for us
but communes
with auto-banks and late-night taxis.
The unbeliever's moon,

shadowing the locked church,
the moon returned
off Cavehill tennis courts –
particular moon

becoming the universal.

Also the tracker moon,
and the moon that is keeping an eye,
and the absolute moon
that makes, on its night, unthinkable
a moonless sky.

But most the unblinking, ancient moon of spring,
making light of winter,
that hangs now in our windows,
spring-restored –
the moon in bloom, precarious and assured.

Lammas Fair Ballycastle
Photographs by Alastair McCook

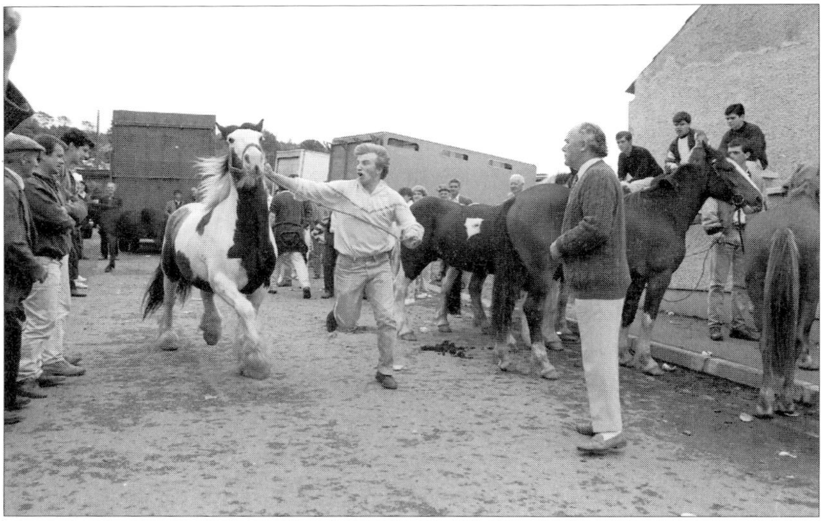

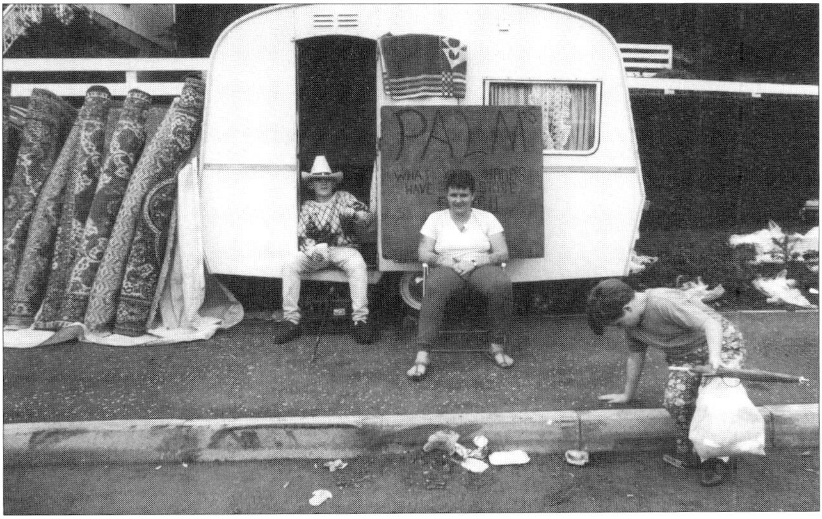
PALM

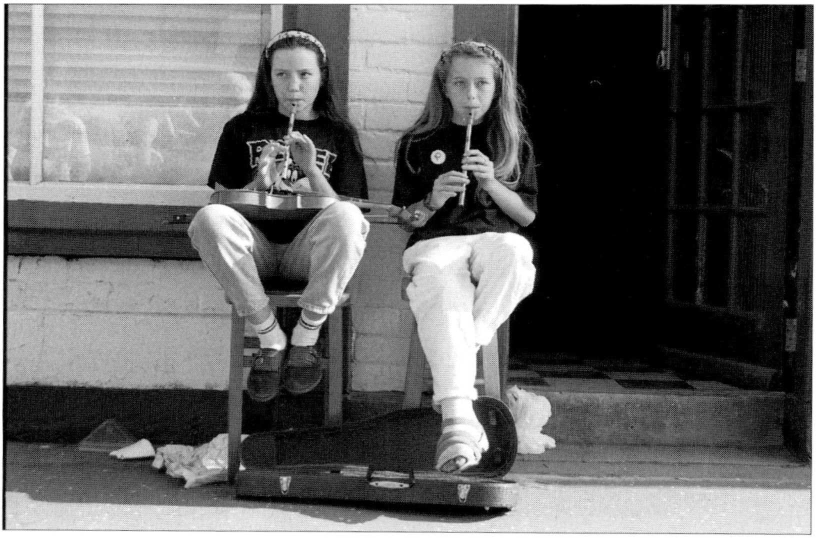

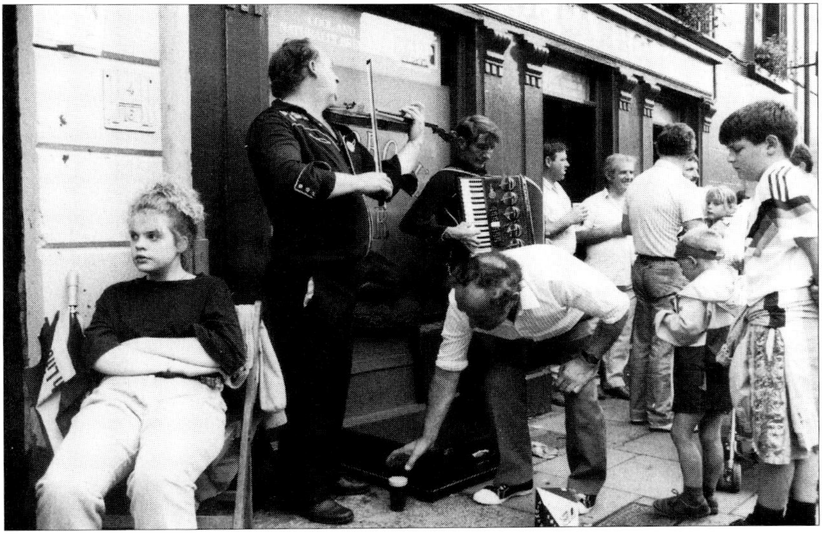

Try our HOT Dogs
FISH & Chips
Burgers Pasties
Hot & Cold Drinks
Freshly Fried for You

Fred Johnston

The Lighthouse Buyer

He sought the certainty of water,
The distance water made between
One shore and the next,
This rat-thick island and its derelict keeper's house
And a blind light long gone out.

He longed to row there on days
When no distance was far enough:
He would go out on some pretext
Or other culled from a lifetime of making things up,
Bring with him sandwiches, a flask, a plastic cup.

All to put the ocean in front of him,
Wide, curved, blue and hopelessly
Indifferent, what land there was
Under him like an unsteady raft, the lighthouse a mast
And himself the sail, filling, flailing, tied fast.

The island stayed beyond him,
More than his reach, out-distancing him
Moving under its own will
Without help from him or any part of him –
One day he looked and the lighthouse was gone.

Big machines crossed a man-built ford,
Bragging in coughy voices they levelled it:
What dreaming there was they put an end to brutally:
Like a gaoler shaking a condemned man awake
They opened his eyes and watched his heart break.

Or so it seemed to him, dog and all
Strolling the Sunday prom with a view of the hills:
Where the lighthouse had been
Was a sewerage plant shining like God's seraphim
Pumps and other engines singing on the water like a hymn.

Brian McAvera

On the Making of a Playwright

When I first started to write plays, I didn't really think about it. Ever since I could remember, I had written. At primary school, in the fifties – and the class size was fifty-four – when the master had singled out a story of mine for praise, what I noticed in retrospect was that he had singled out aspects of my use of language – a simple form of literary criticism really – and I remember the sensation of myself being outside myself, looking down at myself, and thinking 'I'm rather good at this!'

Despite the fact that there were no books in the house, I had read from an early age. This was because of our neighbour, Mr Farrelly, a senior civil servant, who was given to working in his garden. On one particular day I was torturing him as he attempted to plant a rose bush:

    Me: What are you doing?
    He: Digging a hole.
    Me: Why are you digging a hole?
    He: To plant a rose bush.
    Me: Why are you planting a rose bush?
    He: Because I want to.
    Me: Why do you want to plant a rose bush?

After several hours of this kind of interrogation – which might have come in useful if I had joined the British Army and been posted to Belfast in the Seventies – he gave in and asked if I would like to come into his house and have some lemonade. He must have been a very patient man. But when I went into the house – and I can still see the living room vividly – what I noticed was the shelves upon shelves of books. Obviously I was a curious little bugger, but quite what the attraction of these strange objects was, for a four-year-old boy, I have yet to fathom. All I know is that I was fascinated, and that Mr Farrelly, instead of shooing me away from his precious collection, let me look at the bindings, run my fingers along the crisp white pages, flick through them… Dickens in pleasant, solid editions, thick anthologies of ghost stories, westerns, comic tales, the works of Nathaniel Hawthorne and Edgar Allan Poe, amongst many others.

By the time I was nine I had read my way through his shelves. I can remember the pleasure of coming across the thick mnemonic words 'ingress' and 'egress' in a story by Poe and figuring out, long before I was assaulted by a Latin teacher, that they meant entrance and exit. Words were important. They could be played with. And, as the novelist John McGahern once remarked, they had personalities. Words also meant power. They marked you out and, in a world of bigger, often dumber boys, they could gain you respect.

Mister Farrelly only once suggested that I should not read something, and that was on that first day inside his house when I picked up a copy of Hawthorne's *The House of the Seven Gables,* in a green cloth binding as I remember, and he gently suggested that perhaps my reading skills were not up to it. He taught me, by example, that there was nothing that I could not read: that even a small boy with few advantages could journey to the ends of the known and unknown world. He also taught me to ignore hierarchies: reading Dickens and reading Jules Verne or H.G. Wells were all journeys into imaginative worlds. I remember days during later primary school holidays when, bored out of my skull, I would have read a book borrowed from the local library, which was about three miles away, by the end of a morning, and be going back on the same day to get another one.

Reading and writing: why does one kid plunge into them, and another kid hate them? Grammar school, in the shape of St Malachy's College in Belfast, was a different ball-game. I hated it. With a passion. From the bus journey down the Falls Road, the fast-paced walk across Dover Street (a short cut to the Antrim Road where the school was), running the gauntlet of those Protestant lads who didn't like Catholics, to the school itself where any pleasure was beaten out of you. A priest stood waiting at the end of a long avenue – and he was young – waiting to give you six slaps with a whippet-like cane should you arrive a fraction after nine o' clock.

The Latin teacher, a sadist who was the possessor of a very heavy, thick cane, gave like punishment if you had failed to memorise two pages of Latin vocabulary. I was scared shitless of him. Although I was conscientious, when it came to standing up in front of him, my head would go blank, and as often as not, hours of application would go for nought. The point about thick canes was that they bruised your fingers along the joints, and stung for the rest of the day.

Perhaps in compensation, I wrote poetry. I showed no interest in theatre, indeed, so far as I know, I never set foot inside a theatre until I went to university. But at one point an English teacher, another priest, did make a point of casting me in the annual Shakespeare school play, in very minor roles, such as Seyton in *Macbeth*. I always hated the acting, being far too worried about forgetting my lines or forgetting where I was supposed to move, to actually inhabit the character. What I did find out, in retrospect, was that I had a gift for barbed humour. When a strapping young lad was being fitted out for his costume as Olivia in *Twelfth Night*, and the priest had his tape measure around the lad's burly shoulders, yours truly was heard to pipe up: 'No need to go any further, Father. He's the same all the way down!'

I can't say that these early amateur theatricals, all two of them, gave me a taste for theatre. When I went to university, I suddenly found that the English Literature course required me to read English Literature from the Anglo-Saxon period up to the twentieth century, inclusive – which was all right by me – but there weren't that many plays specified. Then, in my second year, I found myself doing the medieval period, with a bearded giant of a man called Carrigan. One day in a tutorial, when we were discussing *Everyman*, he announced that we should do a production of it, as that way we might understand it better. 'So who's going to direct it?' he asked.

Again there was that sensation of looking down upon oneself, for my left arm was raised high, and I can remember looking at my arm and wondering why on earth it was raised, as I knew nothing about theatre, had never been to a theatre performance outside of school, and so knew absolutely nothing about directing a play. Yet three weeks later, posters had been stuck up all over the Union and other university areas and a cast and crew, some from the tutorial group, others pressganged, were presenting my production of *Everyman* to a rather substantial audience in what was then the McMordie Hall in Queen's University Union. A year and three productions later, I was directing a cast and crew of 106 people in a fairly spectacular version of *Romeo and Juliet* in which a young Ciaran Hinds played Romeo, the young actress who played Juliet was being featured in the *Daily Mirror*, and I staged, for the BBC cameras, a sword-fighting sequence across the top of the Union buildings, and in particular along the top of the outer wall, without so much as a thought for the possible, deadly consequences.

Where does the pump-priming come from? There was no interest in books, let alone theatre, in my family. I had been a shy, retiring kid who rarely made friends, but who suddenly found himself working with large numbers of people and telling them what to do. A similar, but seminal, event occurred around the period when, during the holidays, having gone over to London to work in Lyons' bakery, doing the twelve-hour shift, I had come off shift and wandered into a bookshop in Holborn where I noticed a huge stack of publications called 'The Masters'. There were a hundred issues of this publication, which each week had dealt with one artist, in the shape of twelve excellent large-scale reproductions, with notes, and an essay and biographical introduction by an art critic.

Now at this stage of my life I had never been inside a gallery or museum and knew absolutely nothing about art, yet I started buying these publications, five or six each week, until I possessed them all; I started going into the National Gallery in London, giving the attendants a hernia because there was this strange individual who insisted on doing only one room per visit, and on observing any one picture for an inordinate length of time, often from a vantage point which was too close for comfort for the attendants. Doubtless they assumed that I was a potential canvas-ripper. It never occurred to me that you should just glance at a painting and then move on. I wanted to figure out how they worked, what they were, where they came from.

As time went on, I often found that I would be buying piles of books around a particular subject that I thought I had little or no interest in, only to find some six or seven years later that a play was generating on the back burner of the mind. So why the autobiographical ramble, you ask? Well I suppose it's about the unpredictability of what is called 'inspiration', and the way in which 'inspiration', for me, always seems to be torqued with half a dozen different strands, like the intertwining serpents in the margin of the plates in the Book of Kells.

Windowland, which was finally finished earlier this year, had a typically complex generation. On one level it started with the playwright David Rudkin, who, nearly twenty years ago, asked me if I had read Michael Meyer's autobiography, *Words Through a Windowpane*. Meyer was a well-known translator, and biographer, especially of Ibsen – and I hadn't read the book. But about five years ago I came across a first edition of it in a second-hand bookshop in the Charing Cross Road, bought it, and left it sitting on my shelf. About a year later I read it. About two-thirds of the way through, when he was talking about a previous girlfriend, he quoted her as saying that life consisted of 'doors opening and closing'.

Without even thinking about it, a stage image forcibly imprinted itself upon my imagination. I could see a semi-circle of doors on a stage and I could see some kind of glass box in which an actress was imprisoned, choking to death, a suicide by carbon monoxide poisoning. The glass may well have been suggested by the title *Words Through a Windowpane*.

Another element entered the equation when six out of the eight plays in the cycle *Picasso's Women* were performed at the Edinburgh Festival, and the stage set for one of these plays, designed by Yoon Jung-Bae, was constructed from sheets of aluminium. The play took place in a kind of Limbo and I quickly realised that the director had failed to explore the very real possibilities of using the reflective qualities of the aluminium to create a multi-layered 'other' world. So I knew that my doors, and the rest of the set, were going to be made of aluminium; at least in my imagination.

Then I went to Paris for a month, part holiday, part work, and soon decided that instead of my usual habit of working in front of a word processor, I was going to do it Paris style, in a café, sipping coffee or *orange pressé*, and working with pen and paper. I used A4 ruled sheets as these approximated most closely to a 'page' on the computer screen and I had become accustomed to judging the length of a piece, how long it would last on stage, by the number of pages I had written. Even in the process of writing I could calculate whereabouts I was, in relation to a hundred-minute notional 'frame'.

Writing in a Paris café (as distinct from one in Belfast or London for example) has definite advantages. The Parisians are accustomed to writers and artists having a café tradition – it stretches back for centuries – and so they leave you alone but are attentive to your passing whims. Many of the cafés are spacious, and look out onto a thoroughfare. In my case I looked out onto the majestic carrefour of Nation, which is only a few metro stops from the centre of Paris. I found, rather tardily, as every French writer knows already, that café life presents one with a huge range of passing imagery: a constant flow of cosmopolitan people forever entering, passing the time, then leaving; a smaller flow within the current, of the French from the local district, greeting each other, gossiping with the patron and the waiters; and the continual film of the outside world flickering across one's consciousness as one stares into space in the intervals between staring into a blank or not-so-blank page.

I tended to write for a couple of hours every day, usually either early or late afternoon. Naturally, the rest of Paris jostled around. While going on the metro, ideas would often suggest themselves and, much more so than the London Underground – Paris being distinctly more civilised, giving the impression, unlike London, that its metro is not falling apart – I came across a huge variety of distinct individuals, so that my notebook was often emerging. Bits of overheard dialogue, or the mind inventing dialogue for situations which unfolded before one in a strange language, physical characteristics, body language, intriguing elements of clothing or possessions… I particularly liked the Parisian habit of middle-aged ladies carrying sausage-like dogs in small satchels, the dogs obediently keeping quiet and quirkily observing the human flotsam with what seemed like detached amusement.

Paris café life reminded me of café life in Krakow and of course there is a strong historical connection between the two cities, so much so that Krakovians to this day tend to speak French as well as Polish. Other cities that I knew reasonably well rose unbidden into the equation, they being East Berlin and Amsterdam. Now I knew where my characters were from and where they were going to. As it happened, I wrote the first act and the start of the second act in Paris but then was forced to leave the play aside as I was offered a commission to write another, *Kings of the Road,* which required quite a lot of specific research – and then was asked to do an entirely different play, *Fuckability*, loosely based on the lives of Anais Nin and Henry Miller in the 1930s, which also required a huge amount of research. At the same time I was also starting to research two separate cycles of plays, based upon artists and paintings in Venice, and in Paris.

Somewhere in the middle of all this I tried to go back to *Windowland* but nothing was happening, so I abandoned it. I finished the third draft of *Fuckability* late one night in January 2003. The following morning *Windowland* had decided for itself that it was going to be finished and so, somewhat surprised, I started. In an odd kind of way it was such an enjoyable experience that I didn't want to finish it. I assumed that it would take me about two weeks to complete a draft but in the event it took nearly six. It seemed to want to emerge quite slowly, a page or two at a time, and no more. I should say that somewhere between *Kings of the Road* and finishing *Fuckability* ('finishing' is not an entirely accurate term – I later reworked the script, benefiting from the advice of the director Chris Parr), I had realised that *Windowland* was in some senses about ideas of translation; translation not only of individual languages but the whole notion of how we interpret and or translate gestures – what we perceive as emotions or reactions – into what we would like them to be. I had strong memories of George Steiner's book *The Language of Silence* and had started to read another one of his called *After Babel*. I had also reread the seminal *Homo Ludens* by the Dutch historian Johan Huizanga (author of that marvellous work, *The Waning of the Middle Ages*), which coincidentally had an introduction by Steiner. Both men left quite juicy thumbprints on the membrane of the play.

So a rather diverse array of influences and situations contributed to the gestation and eventual production of *Windowland*. As to the why, the how and the when of their co-mingling, I have absolutely no idea. Some plays you determine that you want to write, and you wait for the moment when you are ready to write. It took me about fifteen years to learn to wait for the right moment: when you don't, you usually end up with a bit of an act, which is soon dumped in the attic. Other plays simply decide that they want to be written, and there is nothing much that you can do about it. With *Windowland*, despite the break in its production, I was always quite confident that it would allow me to return to it.

Leontia Flynn

Charles Baudelaire's Mother

This life of vice, depravity and pain
– where childhood's a remote, uncanny garden
with intermittent sunshine only (rain
lashing the flowers flat most days); where boozing,
pills and addictions, illness, fucking whores
occupy us thereafter to the tomb
(preferable, mind, to being *fucking bored*) –
may be the sick construction of a womb

(for what else drags us here?). Yet nonetheless
on whom, his number up, did Baudelaire
– knackered by opium, racked with syphilis –
turn, we note, but back to his own mother?
'Though meant for gentle love,' he writes to her
'*I think that one of us will kill the other.*'

Samuel Beckett

'Samuel Beckett suffers from, or has suffered
from: boils, odd facial rashes, phantom pains in his limbs,
nightsweats, insomnia, dreams of suffocation,
palpitations, panic attacks, diarrhea, aching gums…'

His psychoanalyst, Bion, looks up at this point from his notebook
and out at the London rain – it is raining on all mankind –
then adds that 'a finger is pointed at Beckett's mother'.
Though, perhaps, of course, it was *nothing* to do with his mother.

'It is inconceivable this is not to do with my mother,'
thinks Samuel Beckett. He lopes the long mile to his flat.
He gives a quick shrug at the thought of his last anal cyst.

He returns to his work on *Murphy*, and to reading René Descartes,
– Descartes whose 'two separate kingdoms', body and mind –
two *utterly* separate kingdoms – *Murphy* later restates.

Kevin Doherty (photograph Michael Faulkner)

Michael Faulkner

Renaissance Fisherman

Skirting Quarterland Bay, I can see frost on the foreshore – a relative rarity in Ireland – and I stop the car to take photographs. The tide is more than half gone and, beyond the sea wall, rounded clumps of bladder wrack and popweed gleam in the early sun like eggs in a basket, miniature echoes of the drumlin hills that rise from the bay on three sides.

Further on, the track ends abruptly at an old stone quay on Ringhaddy Sound. This is one of the prettiest corners of the prettiest waterway in Northern Ireland. Strangford may be the largest sea lough in the British Isles, but along this deeply indented stretch of the west shore, where an archipelago of little islands lies a quarter of a mile off and the wide expanse of water beyond comes only as tantalising glimpses, there is a feeling of enclosure, of cosiness, which for me is vastly reassuring, conjuring memories of childhood: adventures in small boats, island picnics and outrageously successful fishing expeditions. Above all, memories of my father and, by association, of plainclothes policemen and the insulated, barely audible rumble of politics and terror.

I park beside Kevin Doherty's van. Along the foreshore north of the quay he is hauling his rowing boat over rocks and shingle towards the water. He looks up and waves, and by the time I get there he is loaded and ready to go.

On the duckboards there are two buckets, filled to overflowing with fish, and I waste no time in showing my ignorance.

'Bait?'

'The salted mackerel and herring is for prawns, the fresh stuff for the velvets.'

Velvets. Stuff. I vaguely recognise bronze flanks and silvery underbellies, and hazard a guess.

'That would be… cod,' I say, and wish that I hadn't. I know Kevin is thinking what I'm thinking – Why would you waste good cod? – but he smiles and says, 'Saithe,' adding tactfully, 'I think.'

Nice chap. I ask if he minds me making notes.

'Of course not.' He nods at my camera bag. 'Would you like a picture of this bit?'

He is sitting on the middle seat of the rowing boat, his back to the sound, where *Harvest Home* lies at her mooring, next to the only other fishing boat at Ringhaddy. He is resting his hands on his knees and as I look for a composition that works, I notice something is missing.

'We're all set,' he says. 'How about I pick you up from the pontoons?'

'How about a pair of oars?'

He laughs and stands up, steps over the gunwale into the shallows. 'Don't put that in,' he says.

I choose my words carefully: 'Of course.'

In a few minutes we are heading south, picking a line through the yachts and mooring buoys of this most congenial natural anchorage. Here I'm in familiar territory, having made the ten-minute crossing to Islandmore through the same anchorage a thousand times. Ahead and to the left, The Blue Cabin, home for almost five years, comes into view, huddled between a thinning windbreak of Scots pines and the motherly arm of Eagle Hill's southwestern slopes. The wooden jetty reaches out into the sound in welcome.

I cannot approach the island without thinking of my father. He acquired the cabin in 1969, when I was just twelve, and during the most tumultuous years of his political career, especially during his premiership, the island became an occasional, if only partial release from the maelstrom of Ulster politics. I think he fully relaxed only on a horse, in a boat – or on Islandmore. In the days before mobile phones an island was an island, though even today the essentials of the place are unchanged: no mains electricity, an eccentric water supply and, crucially, the kind of isolation afforded by a natural drawbridge which is permanently and conveniently raised – there is no causeway, even at low tide, and The Blue Cabin is the only house on the island.

Work has kept me on the mainland for five days, which is a little unusual, and I begin to look for Lynn. There is no sign of her on the timber deck that runs the length of the cabin, and knowing that I won't be stopping by, at least on the outward journey, I have a fleeting and unaccountable feeling of unease. We have spoken on the phone a dozen times but it may say something about that aspect of island living most often alluded to by others but hardly acknowledged by us – that with isolation comes a measure of vulnerability – that my introduction to commercial fishing on the lough will be tempered by worry if she doesn't appear. Then, as we come level with the jetty, she emerges from her studio shed at the side of the cabin, with Rab at her heels, and we exchange waves. No point in greetings: they would be lost in the throaty roar of the engine.

I shout to Kevin: 'Why such a racket?' A bit cheeky, but he can see that I'm smiling.

He tells me the engine, which he fitted himself, is an 80 HP four-cylinder Ford with 2–1 reduction, and I nod wisely, scribbling away. Then he gets into cooling and silencing configurations, and the fact that the coolant exits the boat through the same horizontal pipe as the exhaust (did he really say that?), hence the volume; and I stop nodding and begin shaking my head.

'Not into engines then?' he says.

I tell him that there is a sixty-year-old Lister generator in the shed beside the cabin, which supplies us with power for a couple of hours every day, and that I do know where the Start button is…

It turns out that Kevin didn't just fit the engine, he designed and built everything but the hull itself: the hydraulic lifting gear for creels; the water pump; the cantilevered cat catcher off the stern (for storage); the shooting tray along the starboard side, which holds exactly the preferred number of creels (ten) in a tidy row and delivers them automatically to the stern when he is ready to shoot; even the wheelhouse, which he tried in every position – aft, amidships and forward – before settling on the aft position on the basis, not of practicality, but surprisingly enough, of aesthetics. Clearly a talented and versatile man. He was a plumber before turning to fishing eighteen years ago, and says that these days, you don't fish Strangford Lough for the money.

'What, then?'

He eases off on the throttle, stands half out of the wheelhouse door and puts a foot up on the side of the boat.

'You just need to look around,' he says. 'It's relaxing, especially on a day like today.'

We have left Ringhaddy Sound by the south entrance and are somewhere near the dead-centre of the lough. It is bright, cool, increasingly still. I count four other fishing boats on the water, all within three-quarters of a mile. Islandmore is to the west, partly obscured by Pawle, our nearest neighbour; a low-lying patchwork of stone walls and thorn hedges. To northeast of us is Long Sheelah, a sliver of shells and small stones the length of a football pitch, which is covered at high water. We often take friends there for picnics, lingering as the little island gets smaller until just the very ridge of its stony backbone is exposed, and taking to the boat only when the tide threatens to engulf us. The drumlins surrounding the lough make for a low, gently undulating horizon line, broken only to the south, where the impossibly two-dimensional purple cut-outs of the Mourne Mountains rise to three thousand feet in glorious counterpoint.

'Why *Harvest Home*?' I ask.

'I know it's the name of a banjo tune, but I haven't been able to find it. I'm a bit rusty anyway.'

'You play the banjo?'

'Now and again.'

Renaissance fisherman. I keep having to revise my preconceptions. In that low sunlight, Kevin's white baseball cap and yellow oilskins contrast nicely with the deep blue-green of the water and I ask if I can take his photograph. He strikes a pose beside the wheelhouse, holding the boathook at arm's length as a warrior would hold his spear. I wouldn't care to guess his age. He is a big man, with close-cropped grey hair, a roundish, friendly face and blue eyes. He looks over my shoulder and raises his hand in salute. I turn round but there is no one there. Laughing gently he says, 'I used to take anglers out in the Irish Sea. Middle of nowhere. I would wave like that to see what they did.'

He begins to lift the creels he shot yesterday. A 'set' (in Scotland, a 'fleet') consists of ten creels at seven-fathom intervals, each attached to the main line, or messenger, by a two-foot strap. At both ends, longer lines rise to the surface, to a buoy, or cluster of buoys, by which the men recognise their own gear. Kevin has eight sets fishing – a total of eighty creels.

He approaches the first buoy from downwind, selects neutral, and walks without hurry to the starboard bow; uses the boathook to lift the buoy and passes the line over the creel hauler, throwing a lever to engage the hydraulic motor. As more line pays in he lays it on the deck in long thin coils in such a way as to leave its whole length free to pass over the shooting tray when the creels are returned to the water later – first in, first out. As more line passes over the drum the first creel lifts clear of the water and he reaches forward, swinging it towards him and flicking the lever in the opposite direction to stop the motor. Balancing the creel on the gunwale, he releases the door – secured by a plastic hook on the end of a length of shock cord – and removes the catch.

If indeed there is a catch. The first creel out of the water is empty. This particular set is prawn creels, and Kevin explains the difference. The mesh is finer than for crabs, the holes smaller, because whether by accident or design, prawns can escape if they are able to pass even the tip of their tails through the mesh. But the subtlest difference is that the two necks by which the prawns enter the creel have 'hard' eyes; which is to say they are held open by fibre rings. Crab creels have 'soft' eyes – there is no ring, and the top edge of the mesh is cut a little long to overlap the bottom, forming a flexible one-way valve. One reason is the two creatures' very different means of assessing their environment. Prawns have long, sensitive feelers and tend to be sceptical about entering a mesh tunnel that tapers inwards and has no apparent exit, whereas crabs, which are essentially visual, will press on to the far end on the basis that seeing is believing – and with luck, tumble through the flap in search of dinner.

Why salted bait works best for prawns, Kevin doesn't know, but the quantity is critical. Just enough to tempt one or two prawns ensures that that is what you will get: one or two. Prawns are territorial and once inside, will guard the creel entrance against all comers. If there is too much bait, crabs can get there first, and prawns will ignore the creel altogether. As more creels come aboard, I can see the pattern. One, nothing, a couple; nothing, a couple, three (a good result). This slow accumulation accounts for the high number of sets fishing. The current market price is £10 per kilo, so at twelve to fifteen prawns a kilo, it's not easy money.

The prawns are placed carefully into wooden boxes forward of the engine housing. They will go straight to market later in the day. As each creel is relieved of a strange-looking miscellany of hangers-on without commercial value (I'm fascinated enough to want a picture of every stone fish, hermit crab, starfish and sea spider, and Kevin is obliging enough to hold them up for the camera one by one), it is re-baited in a blur of fingers and fish and lifted onto the far end of the shooting tray. With all creels shipped, baited and set out in a tidy row, Kevin selects a spot and throws the first buoy over the stern, followed by the first creel. After that, steady ahead with the boat is sufficient to feed the remaining creels off the shooting tray, and they splash into the water astern of us and slightly to port: inside the wheelhouse, Kevin is using the electronic fish-finder to follow the contours of the seabed in a long, shallow curve. I ask why this particular disposition – why, for that matter, this spot at all – and in the verbal equivalent of a wink he provides the comprehensive explanation that this is how he likes to drop them.

The crabs are much more plentiful. Not brown crabs, but little greeny-black velvets, or lady crabs. Spurned by British consumers as being hardly worth the effort, but greatly prized in Spain, Portugal and France, they are much smaller and darker than browns and their shells have a soft velvety coating of fine fibres, but their most distinguishing anatomical feature is their fifth pair of legs, which are flattened into serviceable flippers and offer an alternative means of getting around: they can choose to swim rather than walk; to travel frontwise rather than, well, crabwise.

The first set produces dozens of these swimmers. Kevin wears heavy rubber gloves in deference to their feisty reputation, and tells me a few crab and lobster tales that cause me to wince – in one case, to cross my legs – as he loads them, graded roughly by size, into plastic fish boxes beside the prawns.

I'm trying to work out quite how – stopping, starting, drifting, turning circles and figures of eight and surrounded by white and orange buoys which all look the same – Kevin has the slightest idea which creels he has lifted already, when he hauls in yet another line, laughs, and drops it again before the first creel is fully out of the water.

'Déjà vu,' he says, and I feel a little better.

By mid-afternoon we are back in Ringhaddy Sound. Kevin keeps a holding cage for crabs near his mooring, submerged beneath a frame suspended from forty-five gallon drums. The velvets will stay there till the weekend, when they will start their journey to continental Europe. The prawns, harder to keep fresh, go straight to market.

I thank Kevin for his trouble and he drops me at the yacht club's floating pontoon. As he pulls away he shouts something over the noise of the engine and makes rowing movements with his arms, but I am a little hard of hearing and I cup my hand to my ear. He smiles, makes a 'Forget it!' gesture with his hand, and I try to piece the words together. Don't forget the oars? Don't mention the oars? Don't forget to mention the oars? I'm not sure.

I step down into the dinghy, pull the start cord and motor over the glassy surface of the sound towards The Blue Cabin. A thin column of smoke rises vertically from the steel chimney on the north gable, and the jetty, shortened by the incoming tide, appears bone white under a bright sun.

Howard Wright

Apologies for any inconvenience caused

due to our lack of undertanding, a misunderstanding
of what was needed in the present circumstances.
Our tongues were not sharp enough, our words used
in the wrong context. We misread the signs.
Our fault completely. We are beside ourselves,
and our love fatefully refused. Yes, even that.

Our apologies for existing on the same planet,
but you must allow us to make our mark, do our work.
Delays are necessary, as you might expect. Avoid them
by staying put and keeping to yourself.
Yes, our abject apologies for not telling you sooner.
Happiness is out of our hands. You can see that.

Needless to say, on bended knee we are sorry for voting
in the wrong candidate. X marked the unremarkable spot.
He promised power; all we got was choice. The panacea
of information. Digital opium. Greater access. We all
make mistakes. Yes, the same old excuse. He corrupted
like a disk. We have nothing but regret. Yes, only that.

We ask your indulgence for breathing the same air.
We have amused ourselves and now it is time to get out.
We have our enemies. Yes, cold comfort, we know.
Apologies then for not living quicker, cleaner, richer.
For being under your feet and in your face.
But we are resigned to the fact. We accept that.

Yes, Jesus wept. The money didn't help, nor the wish-list
drawn up or the hit-list ticked off. We know this
and are humbled. If there is a next time, we shall
get it right. So hands raised, we admit failure, our souls
dented, our metal corroded. Fingers burnt, we take
the blame and want to begin again. Yes, always that.

Trailer

Pull: the shoe fits like a glove.
The door has expanded in the damp –
I give it a shove.

I have you dribbling blood
through the seams and machinery
of underwear. The words become a flood.

And the book you have decided to try
is *Home and Freedom – The Gun
in Contemporary Irish Poetry,*

promising much like a film trailer
but failing in what was actually shot.
Here's something by Norman Mailer.

Belfast in the Seventies
Photographs by John Gilbert

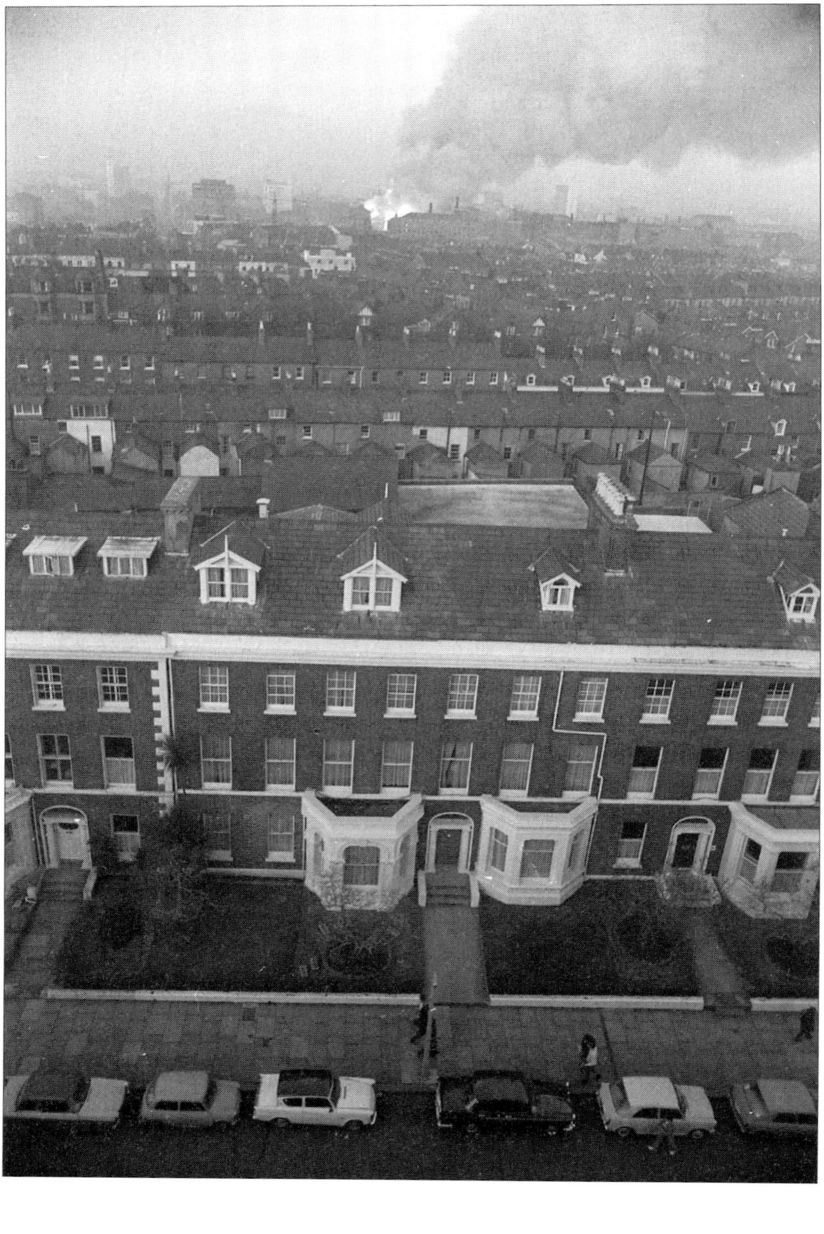

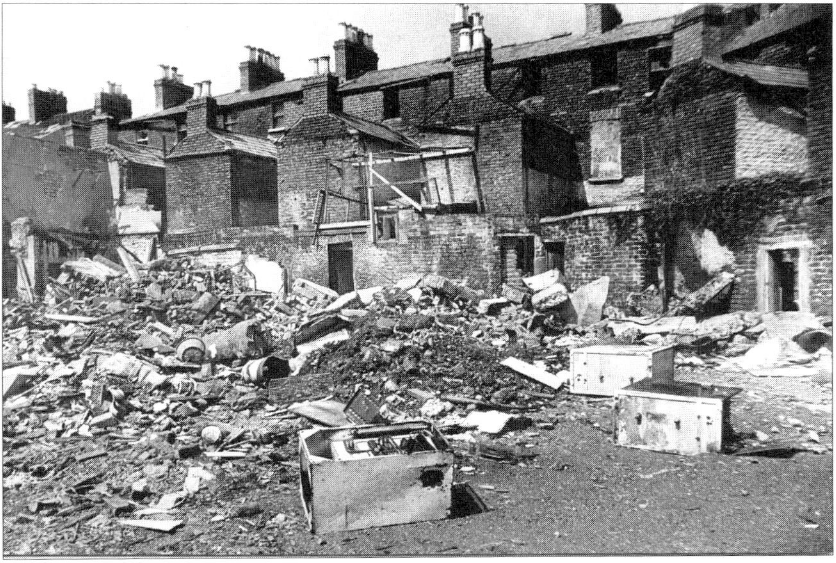

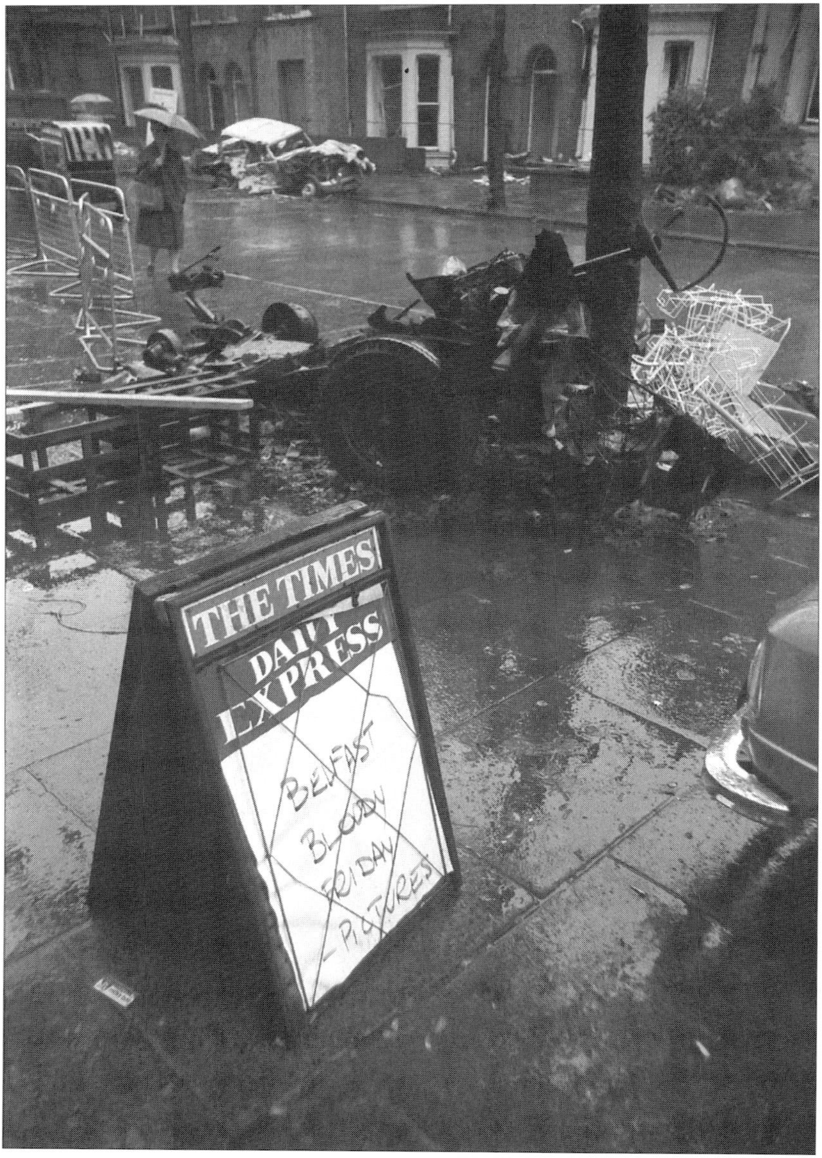
THE TIMES
DAILY EXPRESS
BELFAST
BLOODY
FRIDAY
- PICTURES

PEEL
MOTOR CYCLES
HALL
POSIT
URES
PEEL
SQUARE
99
MARKET
DEAL

Stewart Parker in the remnants of the telephone kiosk on Botanic Avenue

Marilynn Richtarik

Stewart Parker's Scottish Play

In April 1978, Stewart Parker left Belfast to live in Edinburgh. Such a move at such at time was, as fellow Northerner Bernard MacLaverty put it, 'like jumping out of the frying pan into the freezer'. Parker's decision to relocate to Scotland had been taken a year and a half earlier, at what turned out to be the tail end of a particularly bloody phase of the Troubles, and in some ways he considered himself to be a refugee from the political violence of his home. Certainly he relished the opportunity in Edinburgh to do things like shop or go out to dinner or a film without the restrictions that years of indiscriminate bombing had imposed on Belfast. Besides, the Northern Irish capital in the mid-1970s was no place for an aspiring playwright, with most of the city's theatres closed and people afraid to leave their immediate neighbourhoods at night. Parker had decided early on, after the breakthrough success of his play *Spokesong* at the Dublin Theatre Festival in 1975 and then in London in 1976, that he must look to the metropolis if he were going to write regularly for the stage. Seen from Belfast, Edinburgh had the advantage of being closer to London and accessible by coach or train.

Little about his Scottish sojourn lived up to Parker's expectations. Years of Festival-time visits had perhaps given him a skewed sense of Edinburgh's centrality to the British theatre scene, and he felt himself cut off both from his promised land of London and his dramatic inspiration in Northern Ireland. He felt isolated socially, too, since most of the friends he had in the city moved away during his time there. Parker devoted a disproportionate percentage of a travel article on Edinburgh that he published in the *New York Times* in February 1982 to a discussion of the joys of whisky and his favourite establishments in which to consume it, a pretty good indication of what he was doing to unwind in this difficult period. It was ultimately with relief that he left behind what he called in his journal 'this frigid photogenic town'.

Parker's four years in Scotland were not a waste creatively, however. Living there seemed to free him from the pressure to deal in a topical manner with the problems of his native province. Several of the scripts he wrote in Edinburgh tackle universal themes in a less particularised context than is usual in his work. For example, *The Kamikaze Ground Staff Reunion Dinner*, an award-winning radio play produced at the BBC studios in Edinburgh by Robert Cooper of BBC Northern Ireland, employed actors with a variety of British accents to portray characters who were ostensibly Japanese. *Nightshade*, a stage play that premiered during the 1980 Dublin Theatre Festival in a production directed by Chris Parr (then artistic director of Edinburgh's Traverse Theatre Club), is set indeterminately in 'a city within the British Isles' in 'the immediate future' and uses the story of an undertaker who cannot come to terms with his own loss to explore issues of death and grief. And *Pratt's Fall*, the only one of Parker's plays to premiere in Scotland, features English, Scottish and Welsh characters in addition to Irish ones.

The production history of *Pratt's Fall* illustrates a central feature of Parker's play-writing career – his remarkably bad luck with stage plays. Productions of his television and radio plays tended to proceed fairly uneventfully, but theatrical productions were usually touch and go from beginning to end. In part this was a function of the demands his writing made on actors and production teams – characters in his plays sing, dance, play instruments, do magic tricks, ride unicycles and recite page-long speeches in a variety of theatrical styles – but even in the case of works like *Pratt's Fall*, which requires no such specialised skills, getting one of Parker's plays mounted in such a way as to show off the merits of the script generally required a special alignment of the stars. This was not always forthcoming.

Pratt's Fall was originally commissioned by the Hampstead Theatre in London, and one of Parker's goals was to write something that would have general, West End-type appeal. The Hampstead passed on his completed script, however, on the grounds that there was not enough action. Parker then tried the Abbey's Peacock Theatre in Dublin, which rejected *Pratt's Fall* as insufficiently Irish. After enormous angst and rejections from several other theatres (with the 'intellectual' theatres judging the play to be too West End and the unsubsidised theatres deeming it too intellectual), Glasgow Theatre Club put the play on at the Tron in early 1983.

The Tron production was directed by John Bruce, who had done a masterful job directing Parker's television film *Iris in the Traffic, Ruby in the Rain* in 1981. His work on *Pratt's Fall*, however, was described by several reviewers as oddly tentative. Bruce's lack of confidence probably stemmed from the fact that, although he was a distinguished television director, he had almost no professional theatrical experience. Under normal circumstances he could have counted on extensive input and assistance from Parker, but their personal and working relationship had been greatly complicated the previous summer when both of their long-troubled marriages broke apart shortly after Parker confessed to Bruce's wife Lesley that he had fallen in love with her. The two men had arranged the *Pratt's Fall* collaboration partly in order to prove that they could still work together, a determination that turned out to be more high-minded than practical.

After its initial Glasgow run the play was performed by a short-lived Irish touring company in the summer of 1983 and given a staged reading in Boston some time later, but otherwise it more or less sunk without a trace. Producer Eddie Kulukundis took an interest and tried to arrange a production that might transfer to the West End, but he was unable to get a theatre, a leading man, and a leading woman committed to the script at the same time. Thus what could have been the biggest break of Parker's career turned into yet another bust.

The obscurity of *Pratt's Fall* is a pity, since it deals with topics of continued relevance. In addition to being a meditation on the unpredictable power of love (a subject much on Parker's mind, albeit unconsciously, while he was writing the play in 1981), the play raises questions about the nature and importance of faith in a world increasingly suspicious of it. Parker himself had given up organised religion as a teenager, but, despite his scepticism, religious imagery continued to haunt his writing. An amputee, Parker in one of his notebooks compared the religious impulse to phantom pain: 'Nerve-ends tingling with the sensation of a faculty no longer there'. One danger he saw in this rootless religious sensibility was that of adopting a sentimental attitude toward belief – self-indulgent 'nostalgia for faith', as one of the characters puts it in *Pratt's Fall*, which both critiques the hollowness of modern, secular culture and warns against the pitfall of trying to recapture faith through imitation.

In *Pratt's Fall* Parker pays homage to the religious influences that shaped his early aesthetic education. His childhood home was largely devoid of books, and the liturgy of the Church of Ireland parish of St Brendan the Navigator in Sydenham, which Parker's family attended, exposed the nascent writer to the possibilities of the English language. The story of St Brendan also captured his imagination. Like other Irish monks of his time, Brendan, a sixth-century abbot, made missionary voyages throughout the British Isles. He became known as *the* seafarer through the *Navigatio Sancti Brendani Abbatis*, a Latin poem dating from at least the ninth century that was hugely popular in medieval Europe. This Voyage of St Brendan, a Christian example of the Irish imramm, or voyage tale, relates how St Brendan and a crew of monks sailed the ocean for seven years, surviving a series of adventures to reach the Promised Land of the Saints.

Speculation about the real-world position of the Promised Land of the Saints was reflected in the Island of Brendan that features on so many medieval and Renaissance maps and charts and continued into Parker's lifetime, when much of it centred on whether Irish monks might have reached North America centuries before either the Vikings or Christopher Columbus. For instance, a 1962 book, *Land to the West* by Geoffrey Ashe, suggested actual routes for the voyages of the *Navigatio*. In the 1970s, Tim Severin, an adventurer and popular historian of exploration, was inspired to try to recreate St Brendan's legendary wanderings when his wife made the observation that the *Navigatio*, in addition to its fantastic elements, contained a wealth of what sounded like practical detail about the construction of the saint's curragh and the geography of the places he visited. Over the course of two trips in 1976 and 1977, he and a small crew managed to cross the Atlantic in a leather boat built to medieval specifications and appropriately named *Brendan*. The project aroused intense public interest, especially in Ireland, and Severin documented their journey in a film, which Parker watched on television in July 1978, and a book, *The Brendan Voyage* (1978), which Parker read in July 1980 as part of his research for *Pratt's Fall*.

The discovery of a map of part of the North American coastline visited by Irish monks, ostensibly drawn in the ninth century, when Viking raids were distracting them from voyaging, is the event that initiates the action in Parker's play. *Pratt's Fall* was conceived when he decided to combine the Brendan material with another subject that fascinated him – old maps. Probably some time in late summer 1976, Parker jotted in his notebook the germ of a play he then called *Cartography*: 'map controversy of the Brendan voyage, based on the Vinland story'.

Debate over the so-called Vinland Map was still fresh when Parker was planning and writing his play. On the eve of Columbus Day in 1965, Yale University Press published a book in conjunction with the announcement by Yale that it had purchased a manuscript world map depicting an uncannily accurate Greenland and an insular Vinland, a part of North America described in two separate saga accounts as having been visited by the Norse around 1000. The map did not prove that Vikings reached America before Columbus, but if accepted as genuine it would force the rewriting of cartographical history. The 1440 date ascribed to the map on the basis of the manuscript documents that accompanied it would make it 150 years older than the earliest extant map showing Norse contacts west of Greenland.

Claims made on the Vinland Map's behalf were quickly challenged. The authors of the Yale volume – R.A. Skelton, superintendent of maps at the British Museum; George D. Painter, assistant keeper of incunabula in the British Museum's Department of Printed Books; and Thomas E. Marston, curator of medieval and Renaissance manuscripts at Yale – were well-regarded in their respective fields, but none was an expert on medieval manuscript maps or Norse culture specifically. It seemed to many at the time and later that they had been less intent on a rigorous examination of the evidence for and against the map than on building a case for it. This singleness of purpose allowed them to gloss over difficulties that could have been insurmountable, such as the lack of a known provenance, or place of origin, for the map.

The British Museum had declined an opportunity to buy the Vinland Map before Yale ever saw it, and much of the early criticism of the Yale volume came from British scholars. In 1974, when chemists in Chicago revealed that they had tested the map's ink and found it contained a modern element not readily available until about 1923, the announcement provoked another round of stories in newspapers such as the *Observer* and the *Sunday*

Times. Helen Wallis, who inherited the title of superintendent of maps after Skelton's death in 1970, convened a symposium in response to the ink revelations, which once again aired but did not allay doubts about the map.

In writing *Pratt's Fall*, Parker incorporated many elements of the Vinland Map controversy. In the play, a map of unknown provenance showing part of the North American coastline and containing a legend dating it to about 300 years after St Brendan's famous voyage is shown to the head of the map department at a major metropolitan library by a bearded adventurer who claims to have found it in the binding of a printed edition of the *Navigatio*. Initially derisive, the scholar later persuades the library to buy the map, spends two years writing a book intended to convince people that it is genuine (published, provocatively, on Columbus Day), and presents the analysis at an international conference on the map. *Pratt's Fall* ends more conclusively than the Vinland drama, however, with the map exposed as a fake.

Parker made another major change in transferring current events to the stage. He made his 'keeper of maps' female, introducing a motive other than academic hubris. Victoria Pratt, the quintessence of middle-class English womanhood, seems impervious to the charms of George Mahoney, a roughneck from Glasgow (with an Irish mother, no less). But Mahoney offers more than his dubious map. Like St Brendan he is identified as a seafarer, delivering yachts around the world for a living. He is also a spiritual seeker who spent two years as a monk in County Kerry. He did not find what he was looking for in the monastery, however. In a pivotal early speech he hints at what he feels himself to lack in his evocation of St Brendan's fabled journey, valuable to his mind precisely because it was undertaken *without* maps:

> Think of it fourteen hundred years ago. Those monks were living on the final precipice. The West coast of Ireland, the absolute edge of the known world. Every day lifting their eyes across a great grey heaving desert of a sea, stretching to the very rim of the earth itself. An unknown cosmic turbulence. Imagine what it meant to cast yourself into that. No map, no compass, in a shell of stretched cowhide. The boat you can maybe reconstruct... but not the state of being. Not the unconditional surrender to God's will. Not the wild surge of faith. Or the rapture of it, the blind leap into the dark. That class of a voyage is no longer in the sea's gift.

The seagoing monks, he asserts, were 'spiritual vagrants' whose real quest was not for a place, but for 'a state of grace'. Despite his intense appreciation of their belief in God, Mahoney does not share it. He left the religious life, he acknowledges, because he realised that what he was feeling was 'nostalgia for faith' rather than 'faith itself'.

Victoria, at the start of the play, does not appear to be troubled by such nostalgia. She prides herself on being an intellectual whose sole concern is with the evidence. She will believe, she says, only what the facts lead her to believe and is inclined at first to dismiss Mahoney as a 'practical joker'. Her approach to life and scholarship is empirical and objective, in contrast with Mahoney's deployment of imagination and emotion in the search for his own kind of truth. The temperamental difference between them is epitomised in their varying attitudes toward 'the Brendan Map'. For Victoria it is no more than 'a spatial diagram', 'a functional tool for people wanting to get from A to B'. Mahoney is frustrated by her inability to see that, for present-day monks at least, it is an 'object of veneration', even 'a manifestation of God'. For him, questions of the map's authenticity are secondary to its power to induce contemplation. Thus, when Victoria's book defending the map is published to rave reviews, Mahoney deplores the fact that, 'So far as this culture goes, it's just another commodity' and declares himself 'half-inclined to disown it as a fake'.

In a synopsis for *Pratt's Fall* written for his agents in May 1980, Parker explained, 'The play is the story of their mutual attraction, and the fundamental contest between their views of the world.' When it came to writing the play, though, he had trouble finding a way into it. The problem, as he mused in his journal, was 'how to offer the material to the audience?' He found an answer to this technical question when he decided 'to tell the story through a feckless young man called Godfrey'. The ironically named Godfrey Dudley is an English academic, director of a university extramural studies department. He meets Mahoney in that capacity, is present when the map comes to light, and introduces Mahoney to Victoria, with whom he attended university and for whom he harbours a secret lust.

With Godfrey acting as intermediary between the protagonists and the audience, it becomes clearer that Mahoney and Victoria are more alike than different. Each hungers for absolute truth, though they have divergent ways of seeking it. Much given to doubts and fine distinctions himself, Godfrey envies the others' apparent certainty. Godfrey's fascinated response to Mahoney gives the audience insight regarding his appeal to Victoria as well:

> I'm sure I speak for many of us. In observing that, religion was always considered quite embarrassing in our family, and it was certainly never discussed in the house, all of us being strictly C of E and indeed my father being the local vicar… but then old George had a way of making you wonder, if you weren't perhaps missing something deep down that you didn't even know you'd lost. All that talk of his, holy vagrancy and spiritual landfalls and so on. Not that you always caught his drift exactly. But it was the way he believed in belief itself, the transcendancy of it. That was the thing. That's what was gripping.

Victoria may tell herself and others that her decision about the map is made on the basis of laboratory tests and evidence derived from the cartographical tradition, but there are good reasons for audience members to conclude that she is also influenced by unscientific factors. One irony of the play is that Mahoney, who knows that his own attempted faith is merely a replica of the real thing and that the map he has drawn is a hoax, is able to induce actual faith in Victoria. She comes to believe passionately in the map, but also in Mahoney himself. In short, she falls in love with him. And love, Parker suggests, is the one leap of faith still routinely made in a secular society. This does not, of course, mean that it is always justified – love and faith are both proverbially blind. Allowing herself to be seduced by the nostalgic allure of utter belief leads directly, in one sense, to Victoria's personal and professional ruin – a pratfall indeed.

But *Pratt's Fall* contains another level of irony that renders any such straightforward interpretation problematic. Mahoney, who says he forged the map as a 'spiritual adventure', a 'calculated transgression of the moral law', and 'a satirical deception' – and who may have initiated his romantic conquest of Victoria in the same cynical spirit – really does end up falling in love with her, too. In perpetrating fraud, he at last discovers true emotion. At least that is what he claims, in a final scene between them set after he has spent several months in prison and she has quit her library job to go and work for a commercial map firm. He begs her for another chance, but she, having reverted to her narrow, empirical view of the world, dismisses his entreaties as easily as she rejects his application for a job.

It is left to audience members to decide for themselves whether Victoria is a 'prat' for believing Mahoney in the first place or for failing to believe him later. The play even holds out the possibility that the map might be genuine after all: a 'lecturer in Wisconsin' theorises that Mahoney lied about drawing it 'in a bid for notoriety', and he refuses to deny this. What we choose to believe, Parker implies, is at least as important as the facts. But do people who are able to believe without proof have something that other (possibly wiser, more rational) people lack? Or does such implicit belief only expose them to ridicule, as Victoria accuses Mahoney of having watched her 'make an international laughing-stock' of herself?

The fate of Parker's narrator provides a clue as to how the playwright might have answered that question. Godfrey prepares throughout *Pratt's Fall* for a wedding – his own. There are hints along the way that he might end up with Victoria. He has loved her for years, after all, and they are friends of long standing. It is not until the final lines of the play that the audience learns that he is actually marrying Victoria's loud-mouthed sister, seemingly through no volition of his own. Godfrey does not 'fall' spectacularly like Victoria or Mahoney, yet he seems deficient next to them. Victoria has lost her newfound faith by the end of the play; Mahoney, overcome by love as he never was by belief in God, remains a victim of his own deception; but Godfrey, who confesses that 'the moment somebody else expounds a point of view which I share… my belief in it begins to crumble', is more pathetic than either of them. He has never reached out with passion for what he really wants but sits back and watches the decisive people and takes what he is given. Indeed, when Parker revisited *Pratt's Fall* shortly before his death in 1988 he made one significant adjustment in the part that he was able to finish revising: he changed his narrator's name to Godfrey Pratt. He may originally have intended the play as a dramatisation of the siren call of 'nostalgia for faith', belief in belief itself, but its conclusion points up instead the possibly greater hazards of life in a spiritual vacuum.

Stewart Parker's *Plays,* volume 1, is published in 'Methuen Contemporary Dramatists'. London: Methuen, 2000.

Medbh McGuckian

The Queen Maeve Bridge 1922–1942

In the limited light of the dawn
The sprightly owl observed the moon's
Undulating sweeps on one decay path,
Slowing down and speeding up by turns.

On cloudless atmospheric days,
She could feel the iron sun
Ruby-throating both sides of her tongue
Like one fruit enclosed by another.

The icy worlds of faint galaxies
Seemed to swarm in the spiral arms
Of the Milky Way, deformed nestlings,
Black and perfumed, with very beautiful veins.

Reins of ivy of a yellow pebble
Colour showed her the rare earths
Stolen as lightest elements by the stars.

How these are destroyed and contracted
Deep inside them – the drag a star
Experiences as it ploughs.

The Sulking Room

The blinds of scented grass embroidered
With the lighthouse of good omen
Were dampened in heat – she would place five
Red roses before her as she worked.

Doors must not be shut by her nor
Cooking pots covered, nor the lids
Of boxes let down: the dead brown petals
May never be swept out.

She may wear a marten around her neck
Without any gold, her arm bare
Of the marriage bracelet rotating like
A windmill becoming rosaries of quisqualis,

A tangle of white and pink, the bell-shaped
Elephant creeper, with an extra knot
For the vow not revealed: seventy-two strands,
For the seventy-two names of the angels.

At second twilight she would hold
The lobes of her ears in crossed hands
And stand-sit without remission, not
To live in hell as a caterpillar,

Or be exposed as an old sour plum –
Tree to a swoop of birds. Everything
In the room fell in love with the death –
Lamp alight, that made a spoon-shaped

Group of stars image of her, the slave
Of God's grammar, from the dust of her feet.

Sinéad Morrissey

Upon Sleep

The way the dead sit round your kitchen table, their shoes kicked off
and incongruously placed, their sleeves rolled up, smoking
some sophisticated brand of French cigarette – ashes everywhere –
and then disappearing when the lights burst on at four in the morning
as you stumble in to cry, leaving only their smell and that acrid taint
of their bitter conversation, is also the way sleep is: permanently adjacent,
repository of desire, cold. I would cut off my hand and feed it to the witch
next door if I thought it would bring her closer, but the ghost of Hamlet's
hectoring father could not be held. A music box of fabulous noise
that only sounds when shut, sleep sings to me out of range and I am high
in the rigging of my own inconsolable wakefulness without her song.
Sometimes I know she is calling by the creatures she sends:
a blackened bird with a scar-white face, or a softly fisted anemone,
hauled out of the sea, but they appear when I'm not properly watching
and never stay. There is a shimmering to the right of me, a trick
of the light to make me lose my step, a liquid morass to be gloved within,
and its pulse is as breath, one and then one and then one; my son
and my husband are adepts, safe in its keeping, while I rattle about
my too-big house and miss them. Whatever happened to way back when
summer evenings snagged sleep as easily as a small boy netting a butterfly
with huge skies, bells, a can being kicked along the alleyway?
In sepia, with soft edges and a clean moon rising in the sky
– as effortlessly –
shall all my myriad artless entries be remembered.

Deirdre Madden

Molly Fox

An extract from *Molly Fox's Birthday*, a novel in progress

In the dream I was walking through the streets of a strange city, in a foreign country I did not recognise. I was weary, and my feet were sore because I was wearing shoes that were too small for me. Then, as is the way in dreams, I was all at once in a shoe shop and my grandmother was there. She did not speak to me, neither to greet me nor to explain what she was doing there, but handed me a pair of shoes made of brown leather. I put them on and they fitted perfectly. Never in my whole life had I had such soft and comfortable shoes. 'How much do they cost, Granny?' I asked and she told me the price in a currency I had never heard of before, but of which I somehow knew the value: I knew that the price she named was derisory, that the shoes were in essence a gift. And then she gave me a thick green woollen blanket and I wrapped myself in it, and it was only now, when I was warm that I realised how cold I had been, and it was only now that I remembered that my grandmother was dead, had been dead for over twenty years. Far from being afraid I was overjoyed to see her again. 'Oh Granny,' I said, 'I thought we had lost you forever.' She smiled and shook her head. 'Here I am.'

Then I awoke and I couldn't remember the dream. I only knew that I had been dreaming and that it had left me full of joy. Then immediately I was disconcerted by not recognising the room in which I had awoken. Whose lamp was this, with its parchment shade? Whose low bed, whose saffron coloured quilt? The high windows were hung with muslin curtains, the room was flooded with morning light and all at once it came to me: I was in Molly Fox's house.

Molly Fox is an actor, and is generally regarded as one of the finest of her generation. (She insists upon actor: If I wrote poems would you call me a poetess?) One of the finest but not, perhaps, one of the best known. She has done a certain amount of television work over the years and has made a number of films, a significant number, given how much she dislikes that particular medium, and the camera, she says, does not love her. Certainly she does not have on screen that beauty and magnetism that marks out a true film star and she hates, she has told me, the whole process of making a film. The tedium of hanging around waiting to act bores her, and the fact that you can repeat a scene time and time again until you get it right seems to her like cheating. She likes the fear, the danger even, of the stage, and it is for the theatre that she has done her best work. Although she often appears in contemporary drama her main interest is in the classical repertoire, and her greatest love is Shakespeare.

People seldom recognise her in the street. She is a woman of average height, 'quite nondescript' she herself claims, although I believe this fails to do her justice. Fine-boned with brown eyes and dark brown hair, she has an olive complexion; she tans easily in the summer. She often wears black. Neutral tones suit her – oatmeal, stone – and natural materials – she wears a lot of linen and knitted cotton. On the dressing table of the room in which I was sleeping was a marquetry box full of silver and turquoise jewellery, silver and amber, together with glass beads and wooden bracelets. For special occasions she wears silks and velvets in deep, rich colours, purple or burgundy, which I think suit her even more than more subtle tones, but which she thinks too showy for everyday wear. She dislikes the colour green and will have nothing to do with it, for like many theatre people, Molly is extremely superstitious, and if she speaks of 'The Scottish Play' it is out of respect for the feelings of others.

When the public fails to recognise her in her daily life it is not just because they see her face only infrequently on the cinema or television screen. It is because she has a knack of not allowing herself to be recognised when she doesn't want to be. I have no idea how she does this, I find it difficult even to describe. It is a kind of geisha containment, a shutteredness, a withdrawal and negation. It is as if she is capable of sensing when people are on the point of knowing who she is and she sends them a subliminal denial. I know what you're thinking but you're wrong. It isn't me. I'm somebody else. Don't even bother to ask. And they almost never do. What gives her away every time is her voice. So often have I seen her most banal utterances, requests for drinks or directions, have a remarkable effect on people.

'A woman with such a voice is born perhaps once in a hundred years,' one critic remarked. 'If heaven really exists,' wrote another, 'as a place of sublime perfection, then surely everyone in it speaks like Molly Fox.'

Her voice is clear and sweet; at times it is infused with a slight ache, a breaking quality that makes it uniquely beautiful. It is capable of power and depth, it has a timbre that can express grief or desire like no other voice I have ever heard. It has, moreover, what I can only describe as both a visual and a sensuous quality, an ability to summon up the image of the thing that the word stands for. When Molly says *snow* you feel a soft cold, you can see it freshly fallen over woods and fields, you can see the winter light. When she says *ice* you feel a different kind of cold, biting and sharp, and what you see is glassy, opaque. No other actor with whom I have ever worked has such a remarkable understanding of language.

Unsurprisingly, she is much in demand for this gift alone, for voiceovers, radio work and audio-books. Although constantly solicited for it, she always refuses to do advertising. People who have never entered a theatre in their lives recognise her distinctive speech from historical or wildlife documentaries on television or from the tapes of classic children's literature they play to their sons and daughters in the car.

Now she was in New York and from there she would go to London to make a recording of *Adam Bede*. I thought of her sitting alone in the studio with her headphones and a glass of water, the hair-trigger needles of the instruments making shivering arcs, as if they too thrilled to the sound of her voice. I thought of the bewitching way she would call up a whole imagined world so that the sound engineers behind the glass wall and anyone who would ever hear her recording would see Hetty in the creamery as though they were there with her. They might almost smell the cream and touch the earthenware, the wooden vessels, as though Molly were not an actor but a medium who could summon up not those who were dead, but those who had never been anything but imagined.

   She lives in Dublin, in a redbrick Victorian house, the middle house in a terrace. The front path that leads from the heavy iron gate to the blue painted front door is made of black and red tiles, and is original to the house, as are many other details inside. There is a pretty, if rather small, garden at the front that Molly keeps in a pleasing tangle of bright flowers all summer, like a cottage garden. She grows sprawling pink roses, and lupins; there are nasturtiums, loud in orange and red, there are spiky yellow dahlias and a honeysuckle trained up a trellis beside the front window. Bees bumble and drone, reeling from one blossom to another like small fat drunks. Inside, the house is surprisingly bright and airy. There is a fanlight above the front door, which is echoed in the semicircular top of the window, high above the return, which brightens the stairwell. On the ceiling in the hall there is a plasterwork frieze of acanthus leaves, and a central rose from which hangs an elegant glass lamp. Although it has immense charm it is a small house, more modest than people might expect given Molly's considerable success. She bought it at the start of her career and has remained there ever since, for the sake of the garden, she says, although I suspect that Fergus is the real reason why she has never left Dublin. She also has a tiny apartment in London where she is obliged to spend much of her time for professional reasons. She likes London; its vast anonymity suits her temperament. My home is also there, and I am always pleased when she says she is going to work in London, because it means I will have her company for a few months. She is without doubt my closest woman friend. This particular visit, to make the Eliot recording, coincided with her getting some urgent work done on her London flat and I was interested in spending a little time in Dublin, so I suggested that we simply borrow each others' homes, an idea that delighted her, for it solved her problem at a stroke.

   I heard the clock in the hall strike the hour and counted the beats. Six o'clock: still far too early to get up. I lay in Molly's wide soft bed knowing that in less than a week she would be lying in mine, and I wondered what it was to be Molly Fox. Slippery questions such as this greatly preoccupy both of us, given that I write plays and she acts in them, and over the years we have often talked to each other about how one creates or becomes a character quite unlike oneself.

   In spite of my own passion for the theatre, unlike many other dramatists there is nothing in me of the actor, nothing at all. When I was young I did appear in a couple of minor roles in student productions, which served their purpose in that I believe they taught me something of stagecraft that I would never have known otherwise. But I have never felt less at ease than standing sweating night after night under a bank of hot lights, wearing a dusty dress made from an old curtain, pretending to be Second Gentlewoman and trying not to sneeze. 'You must stop immediately,' one of my friends said to me. 'I know you want to write plays but if you keep on with the acting, you'll lose whatever understanding you have for the theatre. As an actor, the whole thing becomes false to you. But I know from talking to you that you believe the theatre has to be a complete engagement with reality or it's nothing. If you guard that understanding and bring it to bear on your writing, you'll be a terrific playwright, but if you keep on trying to act, you'll undermine your whole belief in the theatre. And as well as that,' he added, with more truth than tact, 'you're easily the worst actor who ever stepped on a stage.'

I have considerable experience of working with actors over the years and yet their work remains a mystery to me. I believe that I still don't know how they do it. Molly will have none of this, says I have an innate understanding of what they do and that it's just that I don't know how to explain it. She says this isn't a problem, that most actors can't put it into words either, and that many who do speak confidently about it aren't to be trusted. She also says that there are as many ways to be an actor as there are actors. Once I said to her that I thought what she did was psychologically dangerous. I sometimes think she is more in danger of losing touch with herself than I am, that something in her art forces her to go deeper into herself than my art requires of me and that the danger is that she might lose her way, lose her self. 'But it isn't me!' she exclaimed. That contradicted something she had said to me once before – that if she, Molly Fox, wasn't deeply in the performance then it would be a failure.

Eventually we decided, after much discussion, that our different approaches to character could be seen as a continuum. For me, as a playwright, the creation of a character is like listening to something faint and distant. It's like trying to remember someone one knew slightly, in passing, a very long time ago, but to remember them so that one knows them better than one knows oneself. It's like trying to know a family member who died before one was born, from looking at photographs and objects belonging to them; also from hearing the things, often contradictory, that people say about them, the anecdotes told. From this, you try to work out how they might speak and how they might react to any given circumstance, how they would interact with other characters whom one has come to know by the same slow and delicate process. And out of all this comes a play, where, as in life, people don't always say what they mean or mean what they say, where they act against their own best interests and sometimes fail to understand those around them. In this way, a line of dialogue should carry an immense resonance, conveying far more than just meaning.

For me, the play is the final destination. For Molly, it is the point of departure. She takes the text, mine or anyone's, and works backwards to discover from what her character says who this person is, so that she can become them. Some of the questions she asks herself – What does this person think of first thing in the morning? What is her greatest fear? – Are the kind of questions that I too ask in the course of writing, as a kind of litmus test to see if I know the character as well as I think I do. She begins from the general and moves to the particular. How does such a person walk, speak, hold a wineglass? What sort of clothes does she wear, what kind of home does she live in? I understand all of this and still the art of acting remains a mystery to me. I still don't know how on earth Molly does what she does and I could never do it myself.

What kind of woman has a saffron quilt on her bed? Wears an olive green linen dressing gown? Keeps beside her bed a stack of gardening books? Stores all her clothes in a shabby antique wardrobe, with a mirror built into its door? Who is she when she is in this room, alone and unobserved and in what way does that differ from the person she is when she is in a restaurant with friends or in rehearsal or engaging with members of the public? Who, in short, is Molly Fox?

Dawn Wood

The Twins Weigh Out the Tomatoes

He used to bring us Cherry Bakewells.
Our job for him was to do the tomatoes.

They smelt exclusive, like greenhouses.
A pound to a brown bag – that was 4 or 5,

and a puzzle with the sizes –
to use the whole box, not one left over,

but we were to avoid the yellow, wet sort since
they would seep. When we were good, we would race,

a box apiece; less to spill than with flour or sugar.
He showed us how to seal the bagfuls between two twists:

whip it round too roughly and it would tear,
too gently and the top would gape;

actually the correct weight of the tomatoes
did the trick, along with a confidence in the wrist.

We would efficiently fit the bulges
back in the shallow tomato box, alert for the van.

They'll remember the quality, Bertie
when they've long since forgotten the price.

Town with Meat Factory

Translated characters, above a sink, have a hint
of red-skied old Soviet optimism, but probably read,
Europeanly, Wash Your Hands Thoroughly;
Report Any Illness. This pie-shell making machine
is set up to dream saving for new Ukrainian bungalows.
That brick pink, semi-frozen meat,
manoeuvred in blocks to the hopper, was reared elsewhere

like these professional young couples,
hair correctly tucked in nets, fingers in gloves,
to firmly pat monotones of pastry discs.
The off-cut negative space, drifts, flour-quiet, entire,
up and back over a roller, then slightly
hypnotically lumpily, since one-width-in has become,
and is persisting to be, detached, from the metal surface.

At school we had off-cuts like this – foil sheets
of absent milk bottle tops from the Nestlé factory,
kindly hung by sixth years in the assembly hall
for the Christmas play (*The Winslow Boy*, *Alice
in Wonderland*, *The Crucible*), or sellotaped in arches
for the Valentine's disco. That terrible, cold press:
layer upon layer of why you couldn't dare to dance.

Ron Butlin

Ticking the Boxes

Do you want to say something – or should I just start? Is that how it works… you just sit there and listen, letting me 'free-associate', talking myself into a state of 'self-realisation', resolving my 'inner conflicts' into a happy face? Is that the way? Meanwhile you'll be ticking off the boxes, the psychobabble boxes:

> Death of Father (a big box that one, you might say!) – *Tick*.
> Childhood Traumas – *Tick–Tick–Tick*.
> Emotional Nourishment – or lack of it – During Formative Years (on a scale of 1–10) – *Tick*.
> Body Language – *Tick*.
> That how it works?

Hmm… OK, I'll keep on talking – seeing as how I'm paying for it, like some golf bore who thinks buying you a drink allows him to replay his whole game to you, stroke by stroke. Just as the world's divided into takers and givers, so it splits into talkers and listeners. Usually I'm a listener – which suits me fine. Standing at the bar while someone trundles on about the state of the world or their garden, I'm quite happy to nod and grunt 'Oh yes', 'Really?', 'Surely not!' – without listening to a word that's said.

This time, though, I'll do the talking if that's what's wanted – but what do you want me to talk about? I've not really got much to say. This and that, I suppose. Things. Nothing special. Like I said, I'm not really a talker. Same at work. When McDougall, our Area Manager, starts on with his thoughts about some Head Office directive or strategy initiative, I switch off and put myself into nod-and-grunt mode. Result – he's happy, and I... Well, I'm being paid for getting through the day whatever happens. So we're both happy, I suppose.

Am I happy? Sure. I've ticked all the boxes on that one.

> Nice wife – *Tick*.
> Nice Kids – *Tick -Tick*.
> House with garage – *Tick and a half!*
> Company Car, Company Pension – *Tick-Tick*.
> Private Health Scheme – *Tick*.
> Two Foreign Holidays per Year – *Tick-Tick*.

Yes, even after all that's happened I can still tick the right boxes. The Happy Boxes! Even when my father...

No, that's ancient history. Been there, done that – *tick-tick*. Three months ago it was, and him up a ladder like I'd told him not to. I said I'd call round early evening to change the bulb for him. But no, not him, not Mr Self-Made Man. He couldn't wait. A summer's day with the full sun beaming megawatts into his kitchen and he just had to get up that ladder and change the bulb himself. He knew I was coming round later, coming round specially to put that bulb in for him. He knew that. And I was near enough on time. Five, ten minutes late at most. I can be relied on – he knew that.

It was him all over, of course. The self-made man. Started his own business from scratch. Paterson's Packaging – 'You make it, we'll crate it.' Every single night it seemed like, he'd relive his struggle from rags-to-riches round the family dinner table, action-replaying his successes deal by deal while my mum, my sister Pam and me sat there, nodding and grunting out our 'Reallys' and 'My goodnesses' between mouthfuls.

Weekends were even worse. I remember one time when we went fishing…

Hold it. That's *really* ancient history – a lifetime ago it was. Listen, I've come to see you because I'm not sleeping so well and Rosie, my wife, thought you'd be able to help. So here I am. I go to bed exhausted, my head hits the pillow – and at once I'm more wide awake than I've been all day. I lie there staring up at the ceiling – my body like lead, my mind in overdrive. I've tried everything – sleeping tablets, milky drinks, herbal remedies, relaxation tapes, brandy. Useless. I'm not worrying or anything – just can't sleep. I get one to two hours at most, and come morning I'm more worn out than ever. As for a few dreams to help 'unlock the subconscious' – well, I never sleep long enough to dream anything.

When I do manage to nod off it's just a blank, like getting shut up in an empty box. He's in his box, you might say, and I'm in mine.

That's what he really wanted, you understand. Both of us in boxes – in Paterson's Packaging. 'Paterson & Son' he was hoping to call it. Plan was – *his* plan, of course, like always – that I'd join the firm when I left school. Start at the bottom and work myself up into management, in a fast-track imitation of his own success-story. Christ, what a nightmare that would have been! Bad enough having him bossing me around at home evenings and weekends without it being all day, every day, as well.

So I said no. He insisted. I still said no. Meanwhile I'm frantically looking round for another job, anything. And I struck lucky – the day after I left school I got myself started as a clerk in a factory making ball-bearings. Our motto was: 'Whatever the job, Baxter's have the balls for it!' Make what you will of that, Mr Freud! And now, thanks to nodding and grunting at the right time to the right people, I run a whole department.

Paterson's Packaging went bust nearly a year back, and my father with it. I felt sorry for him. Naturally. Tried to help him, but he wouldn't take any help, from me least of all. Fact is, he was too stuck in his ways – all that self-made stuff belongs to last century. Business practice has moved on, it's all about teamwork now. With him it was just boxes and more boxes till the bottom fell out!

But I felt really sorry for him. I really did. Then, six months later, when I called round to change that bulb for him… I find him… lying there on the floor. Must have lost his balance and tumbled from the ladder. He looked smaller, like an old-man doll with the stuffing…

No, I *don't* dream about him. I don't dream, I told you. Are you not listening?

I don't dream because I don't sleep. That's why I'm here, remember?

Sorry, I didn't mean to start on about my father; I had enough of him while he was alive…

Sorry again, I didn't mean it like it sounded. Fits me right into the Freudian box, that does! Here's how that box probably goes:

Subconsciously I knew he'd not wait for me to call round and would try to climb up the ladder by himself.

Which is why I told him I wouldn't go round until a bit later… and got there even later than I'd said.

Which means I killed him, or my subconscious did! Tick the psychobabble box!

Which is why I feel guilty.

My guilt is stopping me from sleeping. Subconsciously, of course.

Is that how it goes, doctor?

Except that it's simply not true.

The problem is that, these days, you can't open a magazine or watch TV without catching someone psychobabbling about something. Thanks to all these reality shows, to Jerry Springer and 'Know Yourself' articles, we all 'understand' our behaviour. We're learning to tick the psychobabble boxes for ourselves. At this rate, how long before you find yourself redundant, with a crate-load of boxes all your very own to deal with? 'Lack of Self-Esteem', 'Identity Crisis', 'Negative-Reinforcement', you name it. Every box'll be empty, just like your days and nights. Like my father, you'll have nothing to live for. And that's when you'll get to know real fear, real terror – for that's the emptiest box of all, the empty box that's waiting just for you. By then *you* won't be able to sleep either – for fear you don't wake, ever!

Not me though. I'm fine. I can't sleep… simply because I can't sleep, end of story. Maybe I work too hard, who knows? Any suggestions? Any good advice? That's why I'm here, after all.

Apart from the sleeping – the not-sleeping, I mean – I'm a happy man, as you can see. I've worked hard to get where I am. Now that I'm head of the department I can put my feet up and let my staff do all the work. I deserve it. No? If I want, I can retire in ten years on a good pension. The kids'll be paying their way by then, leaving me to play golf, do a bit of DIY, help Rosie to look after her garden… with jaunts abroad whenever the mood takes us. Perfect, eh! What more could a man want? I might even take up fishing again – not very PC, I know, but…

Yes, I used to go fishing with him, believe it or not. Well, one time at any rate… But that's ancient history, like I said. Hardly even remember it.

No, it's not that I don't *want* to remember it. I'm not 'in denial'. It was nothing, just a stupid, stupid … Christ, it was nothing.

Correction – it was him all over.

Yes, I am angry. Who wouldn't be?

You really want to hear it?

OK, I'll tell you. But it was nothing special. Nothing 'traumatic'. Just stupid.

Right? Sitting comfortably? Then I'll begin.

It was the weekend. A Saturday. I was about nine or ten years old. Let's all go fishing, he said. Even though we'd never gone fishing before, I knew exactly what would happen: mum would make sandwiches and a flask of tea, then she and my sister would sit on the bank while I faffed around not knowing what I was doing while he did the real fishing like the big hero he was. Which is exactly what happened. He kitted up his second-best rod (Freudian, or what?) for me, put a worm on the hook for me, cast it into the river for me, then stuck the rod in my hands telling me to keep my eyes on the float. OK so far?

So I watch this yellow cork thing bobbing on the water while he gets his best rod prepared.

It is a beautiful summer's day with reflections of the clear blue sky and occasional flecks of white clouds drifting on the water. The air is still and warm, not a breath of wind. I feel really happy standing there on the bank, holding my fishing rod, watching the float … and hoping with all my heart I'll catch something. That'd show him! I'd be so proud, and everyone – my mum, my sister and even Mr Hero Fisherman himself – would be amazed.

'Please, fish,' I whisper. 'Please swim near and…'

Then it happens. One moment my float's bobbing in the water, and the next it's vanished. There's a fierce tug on the line. My rod's suddenly bent like a bow, the reel's screeching, the line unwinding too fast for me to stop it. I hold on for all I'm worth, shouting, 'A fish! A fish! I've got a fish!'

I didn't know what to do *except* hold on. He could have told me, of course, talked me through it – it wasn't a big fish, I could easily have managed. He could have stood behind me, reaching his arms round me even, and placed his hands on mine to guide me.

But he didn't. Not him.

'Give it here,' he says, snatching the rod out of my hands.

For the next five minutes I had to look on while he played the fish – my fish! – and landed it, all the while giving me a running commentary on his technique. So that I could learn the right way to do things, he told me. As if I cared. Like I said, it was nothing.

When my mum cooked it for tea that evening, I refused to eat any. When I was made to – I sicked it all up and was sent to bed. I remember lying in the darkness for hours, hating him.

But, like I say, that was years ago. Ancient history. Tick the Childhood Trauma box, and let's move on.

All I want is a good night's sleep. You listening? All I want's to close my eyes and rest. He's resting now – so why can't I? Sometimes when I'm lying there tense and stiff – like *rigor mortis* almost! – my wife holds me and soothes me, and I can feel her touch, her gentleness, starting to melt away all the sadness inside me…

And I get so scared… scared that *everything* will melt away till there's nothing left of me. Nothing.

I didn't want him dead. I didn't. You believe me, don't you?

Don't you?

Nick Laird

Everyman

The hellmouth, to begin with,
three fathom of cord and a windlass,
a link to fire the tinder.

An earthquake: barrel for the same –
we gathered stones the size of fists each time
and rolled them round in it.

Also, a pageant, that is to say,
a house of wainscot,
painted and builded on a cart with four wheels.

A square top to set over said house.
One griffon, gilt,
with a fane to set on said top.

The hellmouth, to begin with,
three fathom of cord and a windlass,
a link to fire the tinder.

An earthquake: barrel for the same –
we gathered stones the size of fists each time
and rolled them round in it.

Also, a pageant, that is to say,
a house of wainscot,
painted and builded on a cart with four wheels.

A square top to set over said house.
One griffon, gilt,
with a fane to set on said top.

Heaven, England, and Hell:
the three worlds we painted as backdrops,
when we left Norwich,

⁓

that winter so cold
the rivers slowed to silver roads,
and the oxen thinned to bone.

A rib coloured red.
Two coats and a pair hosen for Eve, stained.
A coat and hosen for Adam, stained.

A face and hair for the Father.
Two hairs for Adam and Eve.
Two pair of gallows. Four scourges. A pillar.

The Year of Our Lord I started the record
for the Coventry Drapers Company
was fifteen hundred and thirty-eight.

Autumns, we'd burn leaves
in cauldrons. In summer
straw would serve or bark.

If the fire wouldn't take,
a monstrous Dragon's Mouth
would counterfeit the way below.

Come the new moon from the velvet bag
I drew one shilling four for Thomas and wife,
and six pence for Luke Brown, playing God.

The Castle of Perseverance.
Abraham and Isaac.
The Judgment. Noah's Flood.

Each mechanical effect
brought bleats of sudden wonder,
the windlass to lower, the barrel to roll,

the link to set light to the tinder,
although no sound was quite the sound –
that catch of breath made by the crowd –

when Knowledge, Beauty, Good Deeds,
would take their exit left
and from the right, quickly, entered Death.

Andrea Rea

Northern Ireland Troubles Archive

The Arts Council of Northern Ireland has begun work on an archive of artistic responses to the Troubles. Recognising the unique contribution that the arts make to the development of a more tolerant and inclusive society, the Council has undertaken to create a resource that gathers information about relevant works and art forms in one place, with the potential of an online resource or a stand-alone facility. Its goal is to create an inclusive resource that reflects the work of all parts of the arts community both at home and abroad.

Key areas for inclusion in the archive are music, drama, literature, visual arts, film and media arts, mural tradition, crafts, prisoner art and architecture. Focusing primarily on the years 1969 to 1999, the Troubles Archive will also seek to reference pre-1969 artistic expression and politically engaged work created by artists in the 21st century.

An archivist was appointed in June 2006 to oversee the project. Research into the art forms and a continuing inventory of existing archives, critical texts and documentation have formed the backbone of the work so far. An advisory panel to the archive has been assembled with representatives from Museums and Galleries Northern Ireland, the Public Records Office, the University of Ulster and the Belfast's Linen Hall Library. At the end of

March the Arts Council of Northern Ireland hosted a consultative meeting of representatives from the relevant art forms to canvass opinion on the potential form and content of the Troubles Archive. In a day of sometimes lively debate and frank discussions, people whose work may eventually be represented by the archive were given a chance to 'have their say' about its creation and realisation. The archive will also contain recorded interviews with artists, writers and other practitioners, speaking about their lives and work in the context of the Northern Irish Troubles. Aural history will be an important element of the archive, which will seek to serve a wide community of researchers, students, academics, visitors to Northern Ireland and survivors of the conflict. The Arts Council will also undertake to commission a series of essays on various aspect of the work reflected in the archive, placing it into its historic and artistic contexts.

This is a timely and important project in terms of ongoing political developments in Northern Ireland and in broader terms of the ways in which a post conflict society reflects its past, the better to secure a perspective on its future.

Troubles Archivist Andrea Rea can be contacted at the Arts Council of Northern Ireland, MacNeice House, 77 Malone Road, Belfast BT9 6AQ. Telephone 02890 385262

Eamonn Hughes

Irish Stories? Filming the Troubles

The existence of a cinema, outside its industrial centres, which can be culturally identified depends on the willingness of states to fund and protect indigenous film industries. Without such measures the identity of cinema is necessarily ambivalent as cast, crew and, crucially, funding come from a variety of sources. The nature of such a commitment in the North of Ireland (as in the South and Britain for that matter) has been sporadic at best. As John Hill's recent work shows, any potential Northern Irish film industry was stifled by a combination of censorship and miserliness. Flanked by bigots constantly alert for signs of ungodly depravity and a Stormont regime that, while aware of film's propaganda value, was averse to funding it adequately, Northern Ireland made little cinematic impression until the Troubles rendered it cinematically, if not in other ways, attractive. The phrase 'Northern Irish cinema' is therefore largely tied up with 'Troubles films', as criticism of (Northern) Irish cinema has to a large extent demonstrated. Since 'Northern Irish cinema', strictly defined, is a very narrow affair, there are pragmatic reasons for this slippage. 'Troubles cinema' can encompass films which have only the slightest call on the labels 'Northern Irish' or 'Irish'. The remake of *The Jackal* (Michael Caton-Jones, 1997), for example, comes into the reckoning because of Richard Gere's role as an IRA man: the 'good' terrorist who fought for a cause by contrast with Bruce Willis's title role as an icy mercenary. For Hollywood, the real icy mercenary, the 'Peace Process' is nothing more than an opportunity to return to an Irish stereotype (cf Rusty Regan in *The Big Sleep*, Howard Hawks, 1946) which had been in abeyance during the Troubles, just as the Troubles provided it with opportunities to make thrillers, particularly useful as many stock thriller scenarios were part of the collateral damage of the end of the Cold War. Hollywood, always loathe to lose useful stereotypes, has not, of course, given up on the Irish as bad terrorists: *Sin City* (Frank Miller, Robert Rodriguez, 2005) provides a literally cartoonish example, though the film is very close to its source in Miller's 1994–95 comics.

Such consideration of images of the Irish is a well-established part of Irish film criticism (in summary: more films are made about nationalists than Unionists, but nationalists are often subject to essentialist stereotyping) and often leads to judgements based on notions of mimetic accuracy. Even a film like *Michael Collins* (Neil Jordan, 1996), which its supporters thought of as a kind of national epic, was criticised on the grounds of its accuracy. The responses to the film are usefully indicative of the elasticity of the 'Troubles film' category as they were, at that early stage of the peace process, still very much conditioned by the Troubles. (The more muted response to Ken Loach's potentially more provocative *The Wind That Shakes the Barley* (2006), which can arguably be read as plea for the importance of reconciliation, suggests that we may now have a 'Peace Process' cinema.) The concern with accuracy is also grounded in the dependence of much Troubles cinema on forms of realism, for which it has been justifiably criticised.

At this point, however, it is worth stressing the slippage involved in Troubles cinema as a way of overcoming a centripetal tendency of much criticism by which films, once identified as 'Troubles films', are seen to be entirely bounded by that label, with the result that cinema's hybrid nature is overlooked. To put this another way, even films which could be narrowly defined as Irish (e.g. *Angel*, Neil Jordan, 1982; *Some Mother's Son*, Terry George, 1996) owe debts to genres and conventions drawn from outside the horizon of an Irish cinema: the genesis of films as well as their function is worth attention.

This is to raise the question of what it means to say that films are 'about' Northern Ireland. We can say of, for example, *Patriot Games* (Phillip Noyce, 1992) or *Hidden Agenda* (Ken Loach, 1990) that they are about the Troubles (which itself immediately constricts their representation of Northern Ireland).

The former, as a Hollywood movie, can be placed in the context of other Harrison Ford movies (particularly *Clear and Present Danger*, Phillip Noyce, 1994) and of other action movies (notably *Die Hard*, John McTiernan, 1988, Renny Harlin, 1990, John McTiernan, 1995; and *Lethal Weapon*, Richard Donner, 1987, 1989, 1992, 1998) just as, and perhaps even more, productively as it can be placed in the context of Irish cinema. *Hidden Agenda* can in turn be thought of alongside other Ken Loach or, say, Mike Leigh movies or in comparison to a British political thriller such as *Defence of the Realm* (David Drury, 1985) as easily as it can be set in context in Ireland. *Patriot Games*, as a film about Northern Ireland, spends more time in America, London and Libya than it does in Ireland. *Hidden Agenda*, as a film about Northern Ireland, is more obviously about the failings and corruption of the British state. It is, then, worth considering how the British and American aspects of Troubles films can be taken into account.

In the Name of the Father (Jim Sheridan, 1993) is worth consideration here. It starts, after the credits, with an image of a run-down, working-class area which immediately provides a set of markers of a particular kind of cinematic realism. I would argue that this is the form of realism familiar from the dominant representational style of what has been called the British new wave, which takes in films such as *Room at the Top* (Jack Clayton, 1959), *Saturday Night and Sunday Morning* (Karel Reisz, 1960), *This Sporting Life* (Lindsay Anderson, 1962) and *The Loneliness of the Long Distance Runner* (Tony Richardson, 1962). Realism of this kind was directed to social issues and experiences and frequently dealt with subjects that were taboo in more mainstream cinema.

As Stephen Lacey states in his *British Realist Theatre: The New Wave in its Context 1956–1965*, British new wave cinema also allowed the spectator to feel a distance from the 'situations… and characters [which] become objects of our concern rather than figures for our identification'. The first appearance of Gerry Conlon (played by Daniel Day-Lewis), involved in petty theft and in inchoate opposition to all forms of authority (the law, the British Army, the IRA), aligns him with the typical central figure of British new wave films: a non-metropolitan, mostly Northern, working-class male whose dissatisfaction with his powerlessness leads to anger, which might often find its first targets in women, but which has at least the potential to be more purposefully directed against the political system. British new wave films are often unable to decide whether these figures are more attractive or threatening, and, as a result, frequently find forms of reconciliation for them.

Conlon's ultimate reconciliation becomes quickly evident at a formal level. The opening sequence (and implicitly the whole film) is a visualisation of the account which he has taped for his solicitor Gareth Pierce (played by Emma Thompson). The issues of audience and mediation are raised by this conjunction of Irish speaker and English listener. So while Belfast is represented in a grittily realist style, the film's form of address, true to its funding sources, is very conscious of its audience in Britain. This consciousness is also present in the representation of the Guildford bombing, shown twice within the first half hour or so. The first time is in a pre-credit sequence (suggesting that as an event it has an irreducible reality which cannot be simply absorbed into Conlon's narrative) under a typically sermonising song by Bono, and the second time is in almost total silence: a muted dialogue track is disrupted by the explosion. Taking these various features together highlights the film's ambiguous relationship to its subject. Conlon, on first appearance, is vital, even gleeful, and attractive, but these qualities are also potentially threatening. The film therefore cannot simply proclaim his innocence, since to do so would be to admit systemic injustice; instead he becomes an object of concern to his English solicitor and undergoes an ethical education while in prison which, as Richard Kirkland points out, makes his eventual release almost a form of reward, thus avoiding the need for a thoroughgoing critique of injustice. The film thus renders the Troubles formally familiar to an English audience, and can even suggest that the Troubles, in Belfast, can be thrilling, but, as if frightened by that threat, it must stress the need for distance by noting that their eruption in England puts an end to fun.

This tension between attraction and threat, familiarity and distance, is a constant in British Troubles films. The opening of *Nothing Personal* (Thaddeus O'Sullivan, 1995), for example, is a classic instance of protesting too much. A visual style and setting which induce familiarity are countered by the soundtrack and a series of captions: recognisably Irish music, a quotation from Yeats, a caption explaining 'Belfast 1975', and another to let us know that it's a 'Protestant Bar'. If Northern Ireland really is so very different from Britain, then why does the film need all of these explicit markers of difference? Is the film trying to be about Northern Ireland and yet distance any of the concerns that arise from the film from 'normal' British life? Or is it the case that the film is all too worried that what it represents is, like the subject of British new wave movies, too close for comfort? Perhaps the finest example of this, and, like *Nothing Personal*, a film which owes a debt to British gangster movies as well as British forms of cinematic realism (the two often overlap in terms of both style and recurrent concerns) is *The Long Good Friday* (John Mackenzie, 1980). Initially its representational strategies appear to be simply stereotypical: the IRA are a relentless, ruthless and largely anonymous source of seemingly incomprehensible violence. As the film unfolds, however, it becomes clear that this is the viewpoint of Harold Shand (Bob Hoskins), a Thatcherite gangster who spends much of his time trying to cement a special relationship with America and turns to Europe when that deal fails. Such 'global' concerns lead him to assume that his ignorance about Ireland need not be remedied. But the need for knowledge in this regard is evident when Shand ends up in the hands of the IRA (which, in the figure of a young Pierce Brosnan, carries once more the familiar mixture of attraction and threat), and the long last close-up on Shand's face shows him rapidly undergoing the education he has so signally failed to undertake throughout the film.

There is a tendency to take Troubles films from America less seriously than those from Britain, largely because they are seen as completely bound up with stereotype. This is certainly the case with *Patriot Games*, though its resultant contradictions would be worth some attention if space allowed. For the moment I want to concentrate on *The Devil's Own* (Alan J. Pakula, 1997), which is of a piece with other films that use the 'good' terrorist stereotype. It was a victim of timing: made after the ceasefires of 1994, it was released in the wake of the Docklands bombing, which broke the IRA ceasefire in 1997. While contradictory stereotypes of Ireland are present – the rural idyll and the strife-torn maelstrom – what remains interesting is the representational economy of the film, which works hard to contrast Belfast and New York in rather unexpected ways: Belfast is the scene of a fiercesome pitched battle between the British Army and the IRA, while New York is rendered as a cosy place of neighbourhoods and community in which the only crime is the shoplifting of condoms by a black youth who was, it turns out, too embarrassed to buy them. Harrison Ford's New York City cop, is perhaps the closest that American cinema has ever come to Dixon of Dock Green.

There seems to be an element of self-consciousness here, or perhaps just a wish to endorse the Clinton administration's engagement with Northern Ireland. Frankie (Brad Pitt) may be in America to buy surface-to-air missiles but the avowed end of this arms trade is peace, as he wishes to bring the British government to negotiations. In turn, Frankie is given a 'good' motive: the murder of his father in 1972, which is represented in terms of the violent disruption of a rural idyll and close-knit family. But Frankie's motive (referred to throughout the film) is in contradiction with the title's suggestion of innate evil. As Billy Burke (Treat Williams) will later ask Frankie: 'You Belfast boys all born such hard asses or is that something you grow into?' The film displaces such confusions onto Northern Ireland when Frankie repeats the old joke: if you're not confused you don't understand. As against these confusions we have America: Frankie reacts in innocent wonderment to his first sight of the Manhattan skyline. He will later tell Tom, 'Don't look for happy endings Tom, it's not an American story. It's an Irish one.' In all of this, the film's main concern is not with Northern Ireland but to establish a vision of America as a simple, good place, where despite his domesticated existence, a man can still do what a man's got to do.

Once again there is a concern with appropriate masculinity. (As if to underscore the masculinist trend of most Troubles films, Frankie's mother and sister simply vanish after his father's murder.) Much effort is put into establishing Tom as a good man who is concerned to keep the peace. English masculinity, in the shape of the intelligence agent Harry Sloan (Simon Jones) is sidelined in the mutual testing of what it is to be a man between Frankie and Tom. Tom is potentially a surrogate father to Frankie and America more generally offers him a chance to return to a healed state – he plays with children and lives in a real community; even his preparations to ship the missiles home return him to working on a boat on the coast as he had been doing at the outset. The climax of the film takes place on the boat. The final struggle leads to the Irish son's death (having absolved his killer – 'You're a good man Tom' – and laid the blame on this being an Irish and not an American story) while the American father survives, attributing what has happened to fate: 'We never had a choice, you and I.'

What the film has done with its Irish material is to make it a testing ground for ideas of masculinity in which, of course, American masculinity triumphs as it must. If British films about the Troubles are secretly worried that the Northern Irish may actually be little different from the British, then American Troubles films are far from secretly convinced that the Northern Irish problem is simply that they are not American.

Kapka Kassabova

Berlin – Mitte

I live in a haunted house.
I have lost my hunger. I have lost my sleep.
When I sleep, my dreams are not mine.

My sense of time is unstable
and I wait for anonymous
midnight visits. I feel that all
that is to come is inevitable.

I have my suitcase close-by, but it's empty –
I know I'll be surprised. I'm ready
to leave my possessions behind.

I look for clues around the house.
But the walls are white-washed.
The ceilings are too high.
The floor has been treated with the polish
of this new, confident century.

I sit by the narrow window
to remember those I never knew,
for there is no-one to remember them.
No-one remembers numbers on a plaque.

I fear they will come one night,
after sixty years of absence.
I will offer them the house of course, the bed,
the kitchen table, but I fear they will say
that what was taken from them
can never be given back.

Mitte is traditionally the Jewish neighbourhood of Berlin.

I want to be a tourist

I imagine my life as a city
somewhere in the third world, or the second.
And I want to be a tourist
in the city of my life.

I want to stroll in shorts and baseball hat,
with laminated maps and dangling cameras.
I want to find things for the first time.
Look, they were put there just for me!

I want a room with musty curtains.
I want a view of rubbish dumps and urchins.
I want food poisoning, the dust of traffic
in the mouth, the thrill of others' misery.

Let me be a tourist in the city of my life.
Give me overpriced coffee in the square,
let me visit briefly the mausoleum of the past
and photograph its mummy,

give me the open sewers, the stunted dreams,
the jubilation of ruins, the lepers, the dogs,
give me signs in a funny language that I never
have to learn. Then take my money and let me go.

Reviews

The Ulster Anthology
Edited by Patricia Craig. Blackstaff Press. ISBN 9780856407925. £25

'Not a collection of writings by Northern Irish authors, but rather a gathering of extracts, *The Ulster Anthology* sets out to 'exemplify or clarify some facet of life in the North'. By their nature, anthologies – and those who make them – have to be selective. And it would be unfair to criticise the guiding principle behind the selection that Patricia Craig has made. Her own take is that she is 'not particularly interested in the distant past', and so makes her starting point in the seventeenth century, in which 'Ulster as we know it has its origins'. The earliest extract comes from the *Montgomery Manuscripts* of 1702 and looks back to – depending on your viewpoint – 'the Rebels' Rising' or 'the fiendish Romish massacre' of 1641, and the most recent extracts are from work by Alan Gillis, Nick Laird, Eugene McCabe, and Nell McCaffery published in the last year or two.

Almost every extract that Patricia Craig has selected – whether historical, recent or contemporary – is something of an epiphany and what she presents is a series of condensed observations, recollections, anecdotes, impressions, meditations and recorded 'spots of time' that will allow some deeper or keener appreciation of the North – whether 'its sorry range of enormities and uphill negotiations… its out-of-the-way localities… all the contradictions and complexities in the Ulster psyche… features that add to its mystique.' For many, particularly those 'from outside its boundaries', Ulster's mystique may be beguiling; though for a few, there can be no mystique at all, if we consider what Hugh Shearman wrote in 1949: 'all down the centuries, Ulster has given sleepless nights to statesmen and generals, and kings and dictators have cursed the place and its ingenious and irrepressible inhabitants.'

This does not mean that the main focus of this anthology is on Ulster's troubled and troublesome history: Craig neither over-privileges nor downplays this aspect. Of the book's twenty-one chapters, half a dozen are devoted to what Cyril Falls, writing in 1936, summed up as 'the principal milestones on [Ulster's] long and chequered path: the Rebellion of 1641; the Revolution of 1688; the Volunteer Movement of the last quarter of the eighteenth century; the Rebellion of 1798 and its natural consequence, the Act of Union; the Home Rule campaigns of the nineteenth century and the first few years of the twentieth; the Rebellion of Easter Week 1916; and the Partition of 1921.' And as current events so positively indicate, the future for the North is far from 'irreversibly bleak' and the pessimism expressed by C.E.B. Brett in 1978 over so many lost opportunities now sounds to have been premature.

Like Craig's earlier *Belfast Anthology*, the arrangement of *The Ulster Anthology* is thematic, not chronological, and alongside the 'politico-historical' chapters are ones on place-names, topology, the natural environment, architecture and, of course, linen, 'Ulster's own incomparable fabric'. In relation to what is now called 'heritage and built environment', there are a good number of extracts from writings about the architectural history of the North. Some historians lament the disappearance, for various reasons, of many of Ulster's buildings of interest, while others celebrate those that have survived – a case, if ever there was, of the glass half-empty versus the glass half-full syndrome. On the literary front, in addition to works by contemporary writers, there are poems in Irish Gaelic, and in Ulster Scots by James Orr, the 'Bard of Ballycarry', one of the Ulster Weaver poets and a contemporary of Burns. Orr's dialect poems, like Burns', are inspired, unlike the ones in English, 'frigid exercises in a foreign idiom'. Other writers and critics featured include Terry Eagleton, Seamus Heaney, C.S. Lewis, Bernard MacLaverty, Louis MacNeice, Medbh McGuckian, Dervla Murphy, Brian Moore and George Russell (Æ), and there are extracts from Stewart Parker's *Northern Star* and a poem by Derek Mahon *in memoriam* Stewart Parker.

The cover photo of a child running down a village street whose houses are decorated unmistakably with bunting, has caused one reviewer to state, 'the strings of bunting… clearly identify the scene as part of a Protestant neighbourhood'. However, Patricia Craig herself has replied to this assertion thus: 'the photograph… was chosen for its ambiguous quality: it could be anywhere in the North, with whichever sectarian overtone you cared to impose on it. But of course it has a precise location. It is an image of Howard Street in the Bogside, as "Nationalist" a quarter as you can get. The bunting is up in honour of Derry's patron saint Columba, or Colum Cille. But I am happy to have the central purpose of my selection endorsed: that the North of Ireland is a more complex society than some might suppose, and that things are not always what they seem.'

Michael Lister

Men That God Made Mad: A Journey Through Truth, Myth and Terror in Northern Ireland
Derek Lundy. Jonathan Cape. ISBN 9780224072960. £18.99. Vintage Paperback. ISBN 9780099469476. £8.99

The journey of the sub-title is the double-journey of an established Canadian author of seafaring books with a vivid pen. Firstly, he takes us through his return as a journalist to working-class Protestant Belfast, which he left at the age of six, to unearth telling episodes of his embattled family history. Secondly, he strings onto this a background of Northern Ireland's history since 1688 to inform his fellow Canadians of home truths amid rival myths, especially that of 'the blood sacrifice' of the Easter Rising and the IRA, and also very specifically of the 36th Ulster Division on the Somme.

These symbols are so telling. I once trudged out of curiosity behind a Sandy Row Temperance Lodge banner that read 'No Surrender. Remember the Somme', and they were led by a drunken pipe and flute band from Glasgow. However, let me say straight out that this book is a bit of a curate's egg. The good parts are the authenticity and Lundy's desire to be even-handed, but personal authenticity and a dramatising style can be a bad recipe for historical accuracy. The book is best read as meeting the preconceptions of Canadians influenced by American-Irish mythology south of that border. The British reader may find some of the long historical digressions from the personal narrative overly familiar, even irritating, and finally, especially for Scotland, off-target.

The author's name is a good reason to pull together family and national history (whatever is the nation). The *Oxford Companion to Irish History* tells us that 'Lundy' survives in Unionist rhetoric as a synonym for 'traitor', his effigy being burned annually by the Apprentice Boys of Londonderry cum Derry. Derek Lundy attends one of these burnings of Lieutenant-Colonel Robert Lundy, the Scottish governor of the town who advised surrender in 1688 after his local force had run away from James II's Catholic army. When Derek Lundy visits the Apprentice Boys' Hall, the hard men ask if he is a descendant. He says it is possible. The name is not common. He had his grandfather Billy's Orange sash, Lodge regalia and military medals, so perhaps these made this Lundy appear no 'Lundy' in that sanctuary of a bitter minority – literally a sanctuary, it being well-guarded by the police.

Men That God Made Mad is a reflection on the stories of three men: Robert

Lundy – a sensible professional soldier, for it seems that only young fanatics would attempt an almost hopeless resistance with the attendant risk of massacre rather than terms; William Steel Dickson, a Presbyterian minister (and another Scot), who was arbitrarily arrested in 1798, even though he took no part in the Rising but had spoken up for Catholic emancipation; and lastly the author's fierce and crude grandfather, Billy Lundy, who survived the Somme to enjoy a bigoted working-man's life of hatred towards all Papishes. Their stories symbolise well enough what had happened and can happen. Myths are challenged. That shouts at us on the cover of the book. The author quotes Brian Friel: 'perhaps the most important thing is not the accurate memory but the successful invention'; and also the historian T.W. Moody: 'it is not history but Irish mythology that has been ruinous to us'. But these well-chosen wise words become somewhat coarsened by the author's addiction to the 'he must have thought as he wrote' school of imaginative reconstruction.

Yet demythologisers who are not historians can get trapped in counter-mythologies. The United Irishmen of 1798 are now commonly re-imagined, as by John Hume, as Catholic and Protestant side by side. But relative proportions were somewhat different, and so were the motives. The might-have-been was not what happened. Despite his true and vivid sketches of the depth of mutual hatreds right up to today, the author seems to think that the Protestants of the North are really Irish and one day will see it that way. The damnable trouble is that they are strongly and sincerely British, in a sense now embarrassing to most British, especially in Scotland. The English public might cheerfully throw them overboard; but in Scotland the origins and Britishness of Ulster loyalists are too painful to think about – the parties are silent. Through grandfather Billy's eyes, the betrayal of the North by Britain began decisively in the years 1918 to 1922. But while social history is all very well, a glance at high politics should have reminded Lundy that the Conservative and Unionist Party was true to its name right up to the fall of the gentlemanly establishment of the O'Neills and Faulkners, who had sent their sort to Westminster as Conservatives, right up until the Workers' Strike of 1974.

That the British paratroops got out of hand on Bloody Sunday is clear, but who fired first is not. Lundy falls over backwards to swallow the Nationalist version of pure innocence. Concepts are used melodramatically rather than precisely, as when the famine of 1848 becomes 'holocaust'. This sits badly beside his just perception of how similar are the day-to-day cultures of working-class

Prod and Taig, and his quoting Freud on 'the narcissism of small differences'. Sweeping generalisations are part of imaginative reconstruction. The aim of the IRA 'was to shoot and bomb the Prods of the North into a United Ireland against their will'. The more possible and less self-defeating aim of terror was surely to break the nerve of the Brits and the security forces. Violence stiffened the resistance of the UDA, who in one terrible year gave the IRA 'as good as they got', actually 'better'. And if a small fact gets reversed in popularising it can breed scepticism about the rest. Many historical records were lost in the civil war, 'when anti-treaty gunmen blew up the Four Courts in Dublin'. In fact the IRA were defending the Four Courts and a shell from the Free-Staters across the Liffy landed in the Record Room, where they had stored ammunition.

Perhaps I am being unfair. The author has used his very name and popular style to get Canadian readers to understand, better than most Americans do, the two sides of the story and the different stories of the two sides. But don't we here know most of this already? And aren't we likely to be more sceptical than he, that the island of Ireland is naturally one state, and therefore is somehow (teleologically) moving that way?

Bernard Crick

Devolution and Identity
Eds. John Wilson and Karyn Stapleton. Ashgate. ISBN 978075464479. £55

This collection of academic papers sets out to explore 'the impact of [devolution] on issues of personal and group identity' throughout the United Kingdom, from a social sciences perspective. As editors John Wilson and Karyn Stapleton point out, there is a rapidly growing field of research relating to devolution. While prior academic work has usually engaged with the 'macro contexts of law, economics, and general politics', however, Wilson and Stapleton declare their intention to focus on 'the everyday construction of meaning and identity in the complex of options available to the modern citizen.'

To this end, most of the fourteen contributing authors avoid making generalisations and select only a few individual sources for careful empirical analysis. These include interviews with members of the public, letters printed by a newspaper and conversations with professional artists, and all respond to questions related to national identity in the region/nation under consideration.

Several chapters offer to justify the use of this qualitative, rather than quantitative, approach. Susan Condor and Jackie Abell cite only three respondents in their comparison of Scottish and English expressions of national identity, and deliberately avoid presenting these as representative or typical cases. The authors aim to understand such individual vernacular accounts 'in their own terms', and adopt 'a general theoretical concern over the cultural specificity of societal and self-representation and over national representation in particular.'

Ultimately, the conclusion which this chapter allows – that identification with the nation, as a social and psychological act on the part of the individual, can take on a variety of characteristics depending on cultural background – is one of the highlights of the collection. The Scots, in this chapter, tend towards communitarian expressions of nationhood, often applying the collective pronouns 'we', 'us' and 'ourselves', while the English respondent exhibits a general unease regarding national identity, which is seen by the authors as 'more consistent with liberal values of the unique, asocial and sovereign individual'.

Wilson and Stapleton's own chapter considers British identity in Northern Ireland, with the respondents expressing a growing dissatisfaction with their British identity and increasingly identifying themselves as Ulster Scots – a shift which the authors attribute directly to the background of devolution in Northern Ireland. It is primarily for this diagnosis of cause and effect that their chapter is remarkable. Its interviewees provide the only case study in the book where political devolution has directly affected an expression of personal or group identity. Elsewhere, national identities appear to exist prior to and irrespective of political devolution, which therefore seems not to wield any discrete 'impact' upon identity whatsoever. The very relationship around which Wilson and Stapleton try to unite the research in the collection is thus largely refuted, and the direction and usefulness of the project as a whole begins to come into question.

However, issues of wider importance do continue to arise. Some of these are teased out all too briefly, mainly due to the avoidance of dealing with 'macro contexts', but wherever the authors seek out broader social frameworks in which to situate the cases analysed, the wider significance of much of this research becomes apparent. Several contributors notice, for example, that the status traditionally attached to the individual citizen as the basic unit in society is diminished, as wider notions of 'community' gain political currency. In their analysis of the recent rhetoric of devolved and UK government bodies, Dominic Bryan, Nikolas Coupland and Hywel Bishop observe various acts of government implemented on behalf of discrete 'communities' and the drafting of a Bill of Rights for Northern Ireland, that focused on protecting 'the rights of smaller communities'. The authors draw attention to the 'semantic slippage' affecting the central term, 'community', and the illiberality of this official shift away from a universalist assertion of individual rights. Meanwhile, Carol-Ann Barnes and Arthur Aughey offer to shed light on the ways in which the individual receives group identities. They look to the part played by history in identity formation and raise related questions regarding the transmission of popular history and the teaching of history in schools.

Since devolution remains of minimal account in explaining alterations in national identities (except in Northern Ireland), the unifying link posited by the editors ultimately feels peripheral. Insights into identity-forming processes arise frequently, but tend only to confirm the fact that a multitude of such factors is at play – devolution is but one. Nonetheless, the authors highlight the broader significance of identity studies (which can inform other fields, such as general politics or personal psychology) and suggest numerous areas for possible future research. Overall, the volume strikes a positive balance between highlighting these crucial wider contexts and remaining alert to the possibilities of recognising the cultural specificity of individual case studies. Perhaps, if we must retain devolution as a central concern, then the link posited by the editors could be reversed: an interrogation of the impact which group identities have had upon devolved government might better enhance our understanding of its root causes, character and processes.

Alasdair Gillon

Magnetic North: The Emerging Poets
Edited by John Brown. Verbal Arts/Lagan Press. ISBN 9781898701606.
£9.95

Magnetic North: The Emerging Poets is a diverse anthology of poetic voices from the North of Ireland which continues the recent, excellent editorial work and cultural collation of John Brown. It follows on from the collection *In the Chair*, which is a highly informative and revealing set of interviews conducted by Brown with poets from the North that includes the most famous figures of the last two generations of Northern Irish poetry such as Seamus Heaney, Michael Longley, Derek Mahon, Paul Muldoon, Ciaran Carson and Medbh McGuckian. *Magnetic North* is an anthology which gives the reader fresh and invigorating access to the work of twenty-nine poets, each of whom contribute ten poems to the collection. Some of the poets covered are at the cutting edge and creative crux of a new generation of Northern poets, such as Colette Bryce, Leontia Flynn, Alan Gillis, Nick Laird and Sinéad Morrissey, who could be viewed with some certainty now – as well as doubtlessly in years to come – as constituting an emerging and important set of voices whose constellation follows and maintains a dialogue with the generation of Muldoon *et al* in the same way that Muldoon generation had itself embodied a creative and critical dialogue with the generation of Heaney, Mahon, Longley et al. Equally, though, the anthology features poets who have been producing work of a high standard for some years but who have yet to receive the attention or acclaim which they have deserved, as in the cases of poets such as Chris Agee, Jean Bleakney, Moyra Donaldson, Frankie Sewell, Andy White, Sabine Wichert and many others.

It would be misleading to foist upon the divergent array of poetry included in the anthology any singular purpose or set of concerns. The poetry covered is not bounded by the conflict or the protracted Peace Process in the North. As John Brown outlines in his introduction: 'If this collection exerts any magnetic pull whatsoever, it is simply through the whole diverse, unpredictable range and welter of subject matter or people that crop up when a poet sets to work.' But equally, many poets either address issues emanating from the conflict directly or, less explicitly perhaps, exhibit a sharply focused and self-conscious attention to poetic language and form that is not only and necessarily the obligation of their art but also the demand of hard won imaginative freedoms in specific times of compressive historical, social and cultural forces and convulsions. In so charged a context, choosing your words with precision, care or cunning is not only or exclusively a poetic endeavour. On the whole, the range of poetry tends to support Edna Longley's account, in her book *The Living Stream,* of the North as 'a cultural corridor', as a place not so much of an intractable crisis wrought by ingrained historical inevitabilities but rather a space wherein the breakdown of narratives of historical fixity, tribal received wisdoms and customary assumptions can also be profoundly enabling, wherein not only the North or Ireland but the world may be – indeed must be – imaginatively reconsidered, reconfigured and thought anew. Nick Laird's perspectives, for example, in 'Remaindermen' both acknowledge and resist 'others who know what it is/to lose, to hold/ideas of north/so singularly brutal that the world/might be ice-bound for good.'

So whilst poems such as Colette Bryce's '1981' or Alan Gillis's '12 October 1994' deal respectively with the Hunger Strikes and the eve of the UVF ceasefire in highly thoughtful and provocative ways, so too both these and other poets featured refute the stereotypical expectations and typecast moulds of 'Troubles' art. This can be traced therefore not only in their skilful handling of difficult political themes but also their capacity to write poetry that is just as energised by the disputes between husbands and wives, the confinements of domesticity, the infinite tease of language itself – or pairs of Y-fronts drying on the washing-line for that matter. Most notably, there is a prevailing and paradoxical sense of home or belonging borne out of a sense of between-ness or of being in many places at once that is increasingly less and less to do with an Irish-British collision in the North and more and more to do with a worldly web of interlacings, dislocations and confusions which impels these newer generations of Irish poets to try and make and then re-make their homes and find and replenish their idioms in crossings between not only, say, Derry, Belfast and Craigavon, but also Edinburgh, Berlin, Warsaw, Japan and, in the case of Leon McAuley's 'Caters', outer space.

This anthology serves to undermine the idea – expressed by the novelist Robert McLiam Wilson amongst others – that once the highly marketable and attention-grabbing notion of 'Troubles' art recedes, a lot of writing from and about the North will have its mediocrity or limitations exposed. The conflict in the North did not emerge from a vacuum as a self-contained aberration but was itself the product of a whole range of social, economic and cultural shifts post-Second World War: in fact, the very same set of intense historical pressures which brought into being the upsurge of artistic activity in the North of Ireland. And the ongoing constellation of those social and cultural contexts will not disappear overnight with institutional agreements or assemblies. Most brilliantly perhaps, Alan Gillis's 'Progress' indicts absolutely the notion that a new dispensation has been reached in the North and this poem is broadly indicative of many of the other more public poems in the anthology which retain a deep circumspection about the supposed reconciliations of the Peace Process, of a dark North brought into the light. Many of the poems in the collection demonstrate that Northern poetry is not a product of the Troubles but instead that both art and the conflict emerge from ongoing social and cultural flux. Moreover, the best work in this book shows that if the current Peace Process does cause a paradigm shift, it will occur not as the change from some stock, public art – peculiarly tied to the Troubles as a passing curio – to some supposedly 'normal' state of affairs and an art of introspective, private banality, but rather as a recurrently urgent need to reassert imaginative freedoms and obligations. This is a vital, indispensable anthology that offers the reader a host of important voices and perspectives.

Aaron Kelly

District and Circle
Seamus Heaney. Faber. ISBN 978057123097. £8.99
Horse Latitudes
Paul Muldoon. Faber. ISBN 9780571232345. £14.99
The Currach Requires No Harbours
Medbh McGuckian. Gallery Books. ISBN 9781852354121 €11.95

In one poem from *District and Circle*, Seamus Heaney paraphrases Joseph Brodsky's Nobel Lecture of 1987: 'If art teaches us anything… it's that the human condition is private.' Art, according to Brodsky, fosters one's sense of uniqueness, of individuality, 'thus turning him from a social animal into an autonomous *I*.' It is no surprise that Heaney should recall these words, as the principle Brodsky describes – the evolution and experience of this '*I*', then its relation back to the social whole – has been at the heart of Heaney's work for the last four decades, and persists in *District and Circle*.

So Heaney begins this collection on well-travelled ground, considering matters of choice and circumstance, of response to origin in terms of the abilities and materials that are at hand, or of 'options, obstinacies, dug heels and distance' ('The Aerodrome'). Recognisable, too, are locales (Glanmore and Anahorish) and personae (Tollund Man, for example). Of course, also present are Heaney's proficiency and styling, his attention to each line's drama.

For all the familiarity, though, there is an intriguing unease that underlies much of this work. There is a palpable anxiety in a piece such as 'A Shiver', which betrays a nervousness behind the use of force, merely in speaking of a sledgehammer:

> The way you had to heft and then half-rest
> Its gathered force like a long-nursed rage
> About to be let fly: does it do you good
> To have known it in your bones, directable,
> Withholdable at will.

Heaney's poems remembering his childhood's relative isolation from the full horrors of the Second World War – a subject we've seen in his previous work – now somehow recall the present, distant conflicts in Iraq, Afghanistan, and elsewhere. In fact, the most compelling pieces in *District and Circle* are those which mark it as specific to this moment in history. In 'Anything Can Happen', Heaney remarkably turns a translation from Horace into a reflection on the events of 11 September, 2001. In the collection's title poem, meanwhile, the speaker's descent into the London Underground subtly evokes the attacks of July 7th with a simple craning of the neck and a curt, unjustified statement of fear. It is this poem, ultimately, which best illustrates Heaney's placement within Brodsky's assessment, in lines as exemplary in their weight and beauty as those that comprise the rest of this collection:

> And so by night and day to be transported
> Through galleried earth with them, the only relict
> Of all that I belonged to, hurtled forward,
> Reflecting in a window mirror-backed
> By blasted weeping rock-walls.
> Flicker-lit.

The term 'horse latitudes' refers to a region of the Atlantic Ocean where sailing ships may be becalmed and where horses were often jettisoned into the water in order to save supplies and to lighten the load. In the hands of Paul Muldoon, this becomes metaphorical fodder for everything from the author's middle age to American interventionism. Essentially, it is any region, figurative or otherwise, of foundering and stagnation. The success of this grand metaphor is that every poem in Muldoon's *Horse Latitudes* contributes to it, and nearly all are carried off in pitch-perfect tones of melancholia, nostalgia or caustic humour, as Muldoon's speakers all struggle with the grim admission that 'our highest ambition/was simply to bear the light of the day/we had once been planning to seize.'

For Paul Muldoon, of course, it is not enough that his entire collection bows towards a presiding metaphor; *Horse Latitudes* is rife with complex rhythmical systems, allusion and the unexpected turn of event. Of this last device, the most stunning example is 'Medley for Morin Khur', in which, in the course of fifteen compact lines, the initial image of a Mongolian violin transforms into the site of a massacre. Also of note is the sonnet sequence 'The Old Country', a wreath-sequence incorporating existing aphorism and a proverbial tone to depict a social landscape comprised of, among other things, domestic superstition and cyclical conflict:

> Every heron was a presager
> of some disaster after which, we'd wager,
> every resort was a last resort.
> Every resort was a last resort
> with a harbour that harboured an old grudge.

Given some of the more formal aspects of his work, not to mention an often unabashed elusiveness, Muldoon has realised, in *Horse Latitudes*, a work of awesome sympathy. The collection closes with an elegy for his friend, the musician Warren Zevon, an elegy which also recalls Muldoon's sister's passing from cancer in 2005. The graceful progression of this final poem – in tercets near-to, though not quite, *terza rima*, and interspersed with lines from Donne – are illustrative of the collection as a whole, as a work that painstakingly attends to its endeavour; as if the author, having found himself motionless upon a vast sea, had resolved to engage his fate by examining the depth of the water surrounding him.

Medbh McGuckian states, in 'The Currach Requires No Harbours', 'I have learned to live/in peace with what there is.' The admission comes amidst lines which detail a fractured memory: the type of poem which McGuckian's honed style of twisting syntax, compounded subjects and oscillating tenses is adapted to write. In instances such as this one, her plain statements come like a gasp of air upon waking from a dream of drowning, and much of *The Currach...* is able to operate in this way. Tension is built behind fragmented lines presented as though they offer full explanations. Sequences of colours, spaces, synaesthesia, are the features of dreamlike atmospheres. However, it is this very style that leads some poems to underachieve, as they rely too often on the same colour-descriptions to fill an adjectival gap, or upon innately imprecise synaesthesia to shore up a metaphor. McGuckian herself has described part of her practice as writing 'constellations' of poems around a theme or image, and then finding that one is the archetype, the correct poem. For the first half of this collection it may be that her practice is too apparent, the fortunate upside of which is that the bright nuclei of these constellations are included as well.

At any rate, the latter half of the book takes on a voice that's distinctly (though not wildly) different from that of the opening poems. Pieces such as 'A Sovereign Medicine for the Greensickness' and 'Anne Glyd, Her Book, 1656' present instructions for folk remedies in carefully measured lines, and in the course of

'The Good Wife Taught Her Daughter' the change in voice is enacted gradually through the poem. Sadly, I think, you can only half-attach these voices' origins to an incomplete acknowledgement on the final page. At any rate, these latter poems are less involved with redundant imagery, and it seems, therefore, more assured of their individual purposes. It is here that we approach work that is McGuckian at her best: expressive of an internalised discomfort, oblique yet inescapably sincere.

Over multiple readings, McGuckian's poems open up to you, revealing shades of meaning layered within her difficult constructions. With this poet's emotive facility, there is a truly profound joy in their uncovering. Unfortunately, in this collection, you may first have to wade through some less convincing work, before finding that you can be 'at peace with what there is'.

Stephen Lackaye

The End of the Poem: Oxford Lectures in Poetry
Paul Muldoon. Faber. ISBN 9780571227402. £25.00

First, let me come clean. I know Paul Muldoon well. We teach in adjacent departments in the same university. I am his bass player, and we write songs together. I also taught in Oxford for a long time, hosted Muldoon for his 1998 Clarendon Lectures (published in 2000 as *To Ireland, I*) and was present when some of his lectures as Oxford's Professor of Poetry 1999–2004, collectively published in the volume under review, were delivered. Hell, I even voted for him. And I have a very clear memory of former colleagues being present at the lectures (among them Tom Paulin, to whom the volume is dedicated), of the Texas policeman called Muldoon who came to hear one of them, and the heckler at one of the later occasions who railed at the 'poetry establishment' with the help of a foghorn, while being gently herded out of the Examination Schools by another Irish poet, Bernard O'Donoghue, and the poetry editor and book historian John Barnard.

These lectures are many ways of seeing the 'end' of poetry. They are generally fun; easy and pleasant to read; all helped by an extremely attractive layout. They represent an Anglo-Irish literary intelligence that has assimilated English language poetry, and English translations of poetry in other languages, on a global scale. Thus there are lectures on poems by Montale, Pessoa and Tsvetayeva, as well as by, for instance, Bishop, Hughes and Arnold. The outlook is positively cosmopolitan. Muldoon is no Heaney in prose method, replicating the method of his poetry in sonorous and sacramental sentences. He teases the reader with a critical persona that only a poet so sure of his mastery and his reputation could compound. Long, reflective sentences mimic the critic-poet on a tightrope walk, daring to make connections that offend and dumbfound, or awe (like seeing Marvell's 'Horatian Ode' as the template for Lowell's poem on Lyndon Johnson). Much has already been made of this 'stunt reading' in prominent places, but the quest for 'one skin' shared between several poems by different poets, revealed through a consideration of several kinds of writing, strikes me as natural, and in Muldoon's hands, compelling. He knows its limits well, knows the other poets, like Auden, who were stunt critics in their own verse and who fell off their tightrope so doing.

Within the sinews connecting the shape of some poems with the shape of others, with different lives and with various compartments of reality, one is struck by a series of forceful revelatory passages. These are often to do with sex. There is no better example that the reading of Stevie Smith's 'I Remember', with its evocations of tuberculosis-afflicted young brides and old bridegrooms in bed under skies full of bombers. Jokes abound in reference to works of literary theory with the same name ('the unfortunately titled *The End of the Poem*' by Giorgio Agamben), and the 'end' or 'ends' in the matter of sex or gender, although never stooping to the vulgarity of an explicit 'getting one's end away'. In a lingering investigation that only confirms both the mastery of the poet and the acuity of the critic, himself both detective and corrective grammarian, we are taken to the clinch. The nuptial poem has nowhere else to go, but is a place *in extremis*:

> Part of the brilliance of 'I Remember' is that we may read Harry's exasperated 'Oh my bride, my bride' as coinciding precisely with the moment when the bombers do indeed collide, the moment when sexual ravishment does indeed occur but is indistinguishable from the ravages of war, the moment when sexual politics and the politics of the poem are inextricably combined in what Robert Lowell once described as Stevie Smith's 'unique and cheerfully gruesome voice'. Those interested in Muldoon's particular associations of sex and (aerial) combat or acrobatics should consult his song lyrics 'Don't Try this at Home' and 'Going through the Hoops' in *General Admission* (Gallery Press, 2006), and look forward to the as yet unpublished and unrecorded '11 O'Clock'.

There's little stunt in these readings since they arise forcefully from careful observations of the texture of the poems, such as the unpacking of the submarine 'image trove' in H.D.'s 'Sea Poppies', the senses of precious, other, odorous, oozing, mantic, Keatsian (definitely erotic), rising in intensity until the crescendo acknowledgement of the sexual indeterminacy of H.D.'s identity, and behind that a same-sex desire identity waiting to get out (with two known female lovers), together with some sideways renderings of psychoanalytical inquiries, remote parents and Freud himself, and outreach in a more distant echo to the poppy fields of First World War Flanders, where fought fellow poets Richard Aldington and John MacCrae.

> Let's look at those other two adjectives, 'stricken' and 'shriven' which H.D. uses in the phrase 'stricken or shriven or shriveled.' It's difficult not to think

that H.D. doesn't quite understand the word 'shriven', a word meaning 'confessed' or 'absolved', from the verb 'to shrive', with the transitive meaning of 'to impose penance upon; hence, to administer absolution to; to hear the confession of', and the intransitive meaning of 'to make one's confession and receive absolution and penance.'

'Masturbation', the theme that emerged in the volume has become 'mistressbation'; and language finally beats sex. There aren't many poets who can write commentary with such lightness of touch, yet with the sure grasp of a turkey-buzzard, and still fewer poets are given the opportunity to write poetry criticism at such length. *The End of the Poem* is a rare set of dishes: taste it while you can.

Nigel Smith

The Raw Shark Texts
Steven Hall. Canongate. ISBN 9781841959030. £11.99

Steven Hall's first novel, billed as a psychological thriller about loss and the nature of identity, caused a feeding frenzy at the major publishing fairs. Twenty international rights deals have already been signed and film rights are currently under negotiation, with Tilda Swinton tipped to take the female lead. Hall blogs enthusiastically about his success on *MySpace*, whilst the novel's own site slickly exploits web technology. Frenetic excitement circles around the novel's cult potential.

A promising storyteller with a huge imagination, Hall is young and playful, energised and unfettered. He begins his chapters with quotations from Borges, Murikami and Calvino, nibbling the edges of magic realism, sliding miraculous elements into the basic reality of one young man's life. The most memorable splash is made by a man-eating shark: not any old jaws, but a conceptual shark that 'feeds on human memory and the intrinsic sense of self'. This is some way from Douglas Adams' famous Babel fish, a benign translator. The Ludovician is a powerful predator that scents the blood of conceptual thought and moves in, mouth-open.

Eric Sanderson wakes up badly chewed. The room is ordinary, the man in the mirror is nondescript if a trifle sickly, and Eric is onto his second life. He has no idea who or where he is but he remembers his name, 'a relic of something nine-tenths collapsed'. A driving license supplies his bureaucratic essentials and Eric is left to fight a rearguard action against the shark. Thankfully his first incarnation has foreseen his demise and left his successor with some helpful clues. The first is an instruction to contact Dr Randle, a psychologist, who tells him that he has a rare dissociative condition. On no account, she instructs, must he open correspondence from the 'first' Eric Sanderson. Confused and disorientated, Eric agrees, until aggressive sounds from a mysterious locked room change his mind and spark a dangerous chain of events. Escaping miraculously, with more lives than his obstreperous pet cat, Eric is forced to abandon his current strategy of sofa, mail avoidance and alcohol. He cannot afford to be complacent. With his 'first self' urging him onwards with 'regret and also hope', he has to discover how to kill the shark before it finishes him off.

Reconstructing his personality on the run, Eric is plunged into the story of his own life's tragedy. The 'first' Eric's girlfriend, Clio Aames, was killed in a diving accident in Greece. Eric may have tried to resurrect her by using the shark, or perhaps simply her death is the source of his trauma. In any case, a mysterious girl called Scout saves Eric from yet another shark attack. She is sassy and smart, borrowing his clothes and looking particularly good in his underpants. Like Clio, she also has a smiley face tattooed on her big toe. Hall throws in such clues, floating them in the narrative to be ripped, chewed and twisted. Ambiguity is the backdrop against which his high-octane story continues to unfold.

The only problem is that Hall loosens his grip. The storyline increasingly becomes some kind of cyber-punk fantasy quest tale. If Scout wasn't so busy wearing Eric's pants I could imagine her sliding into tight leather and moving into the matrix, which incidentally is called 'unspace' in Hall's narrative. The comparison is not perfect, but Hall's dreamscape sequences take place in dark, underground corridors, warehouses and dingy places of altered reality. Characters like Mr Nobody (bad) and Trey Fidorous (good) help the pair in their quest to kill the shark and by doing so destroy Mycroft Hall, a man turned super-computer whose cyberspace tentacles insert themselves into unsuspecting brains, including Scout's. Needless to say, he is the super villain and Ian Fleming would have been impressed. I wasn't particularly. The existential charge of the novel had excited me but it drifts to some unspecified point on the horizon, unmoving and increasingly irrelevant. In its place, Hall pursues a love, loss and save-the-world story that simply lacks conviction. Hall seems to have had an inkling of this problem. He writes close to the end, musing on the nature of loss, that 'whatever you write down it's not the truth, it's just a story'. Although not exactly original, the sentiment is rather close to the truth: his is a rollicking read, but hardly a contender for literary fiction of the year.

Although Hall is keen to explore the depths and dangers of language, his original and energetic style sinks occasionally into sediment. Unexpected metaphors, chain-ganged verbs and expansive, pumping descriptions can be playful, sexy and imaginative. They can also be irritating and flaccid, whilst his dialogue has a tendency to read like a movie script; not exactly a compliment. I suspect that at heart Hall is not a writer, but a visual artist with a keen eye for concept. He peppers the novel with geek-chic graphics and a 'flicker book' sequence that accelerate its sea-drenched climax. I was left thinking that *The Raw Shark Texts* would make a better film. Bring on the blockbuster.

Hannah Adcock

The Gradual Gathering of Lust and Other Tales
Toni Davidson. Canongate. ISBN 9781841958989. £10.99

Following the critical success of his 1999 novel *Scar Culture*, Toni Davidson can be excused for keeping his focus on the darker corners of humanity in his collection of short stories. The depravity which his novel explored to such powerful effect is further excavated in these eight stories, detailing the lust and insecurity of his characters, covering a broad spectrum of personal and sexual dysfunction. It is material relevant to our modern world, itself full of perversion and dysfunction, both hidden and blatant. Mr Davidson captures this world in words and hangs it up for his readers to observe, if not enjoy.

Perhaps it is the profusion of dysfunction in our society which steals what might otherwise be the shock value of this collection, or maybe it is just this reviewer's own jaded view of the world which makes the shocking seem predictable. Whatever the case, Davidson's stories seldom manage to shock, despite the sordid material of which they are made.

The writing in this collection does showcase an unmistakable talent, paired with an obvious love of language and a meticulous attention to detail. Prominent in all eight stories is an imagination which has rightly been praised. Some of the stories are patently fantastic, most notably 'The Inert Penis of the Man Who Had Just Been Shot', in which the town outcast works feverishly at a stone monument marking the molestation of a young girl and the consequent execution of its perpetrator – by his own mother – in order that the village may never forget the horror of the act. This fantastical facet of Davidson's imagination is also apparent in the naming of his characters: following the trend set in *Scar Culture*, in *The Gradual Gathering of Lust* we are greeted with the idiosyncratically monikered Rean, Louche, Solace, Minus and Silem.

Davidson's nonconformist approach to literature goes beyond the naming of his characters and is evident in some very postmodern narrative touches. In 'Some People are Born to be a Burden on the Rest', the story is narrated to a large extent by the ghost of an unborn child of the main character. In 'Raul and Petra, Uri and Renzo' – the story of two documentarians hoping to chronicle a tantric sex weekend – both the hosts and the documentarians themselves are brought to us in a documentary-style presentation, complete with scene breaks and an outside and unidentified interviewer.

All of Davidson's notable talent, imagination and literary flourishes come together most successfully in the title story, in which we join a brother and sister years after a childhood incestuous encounter and mere days after the death of their anthropologist parents in the same plane crash which has stranded the two of them on a tropical island. The story of Karine and her appropriately named brother Minus's differing attempts at coming to grips with their new situation is presented from a powerfully omniscient, third person perspective, interspersed with the soul-searching final journal entries of their regret- and anger-filled mother. The language is lush, beautiful and edgy to match the jungle setting, and the characters of brother and sister are perfectly presented through the combination of backstory given in the mother's journal and their own troubled thoughts.

Unfortunately, the same balance is not evident throughout the collection. Perhaps Davidson is more comfortable working in the longer medium of the novel, but here the combination of unusual character names, fantastic settings and overly introspective narrators has the undesirable effect of depersonalising characters who are meant to be sympathetic – potentially alienating readers who should instead be growing more and more involved as they read the stories.

The Gradual Gathering of Lust starts strong, amplifying the expectation created by the title with the most genuinely shocking of the eight stories, 'Affections of the Ejaculation Centre', in which the reader is asked to descend into madness and, finally, death with a geriatric nymphomaniac. Despite the dubious psychiatric validity of Rean's experiences, the sense of madness and lust are recreated in a frenetic, disjointed story.

The collection stalls in the second half, though, with 'Some People are Born to be a Burden on the Rest'. Despite compelling subject-matter which is particularly relevant in a society standing on the verge of all kinds of breakthroughs in genetics, the narrator's dialect – meant to approximate rural American speech – is distracting, and the story lumbers awkwardly to a predictable conclusion. The early vigour evident in the first two stories is never recaptured and ultimately the collection peters out in the introspective ramblings of a lonely beauty queen in 'Miss Globe X'.

Full of talent and potential, and with a critically acclaimed novel to his name, Toni Davidson has not quite managed to recapture the same form and force with *The Gradual Gathering of Lust*.

Andy Gloege

The Last of the Tinsmiths: The Life of Willie MacPhee
Sheila Douglas. Birlinn. ISBN 1841585114. £7.99

In the 1980s and 90s, Sheila Douglas and her late husband Andrew were devoted to recording storyteller-piper, Willie MacPhee. Widely regarded as the last of the tinsmiths, 'Big Willie' had a vast knowledge of traditional culture, though little of his impressive repertoire saw print during his life. More as friend than scholar, Sheila Douglas weaves stories and tunes through seven chapters: 'Glimpses of an Ancient Way of Life', 'Kinship and Family', 'Making a Living', 'Piping Times', 'Tales of the Unexpected', 'The Supernatural' and, finally, 'The Perthshire Years'. Though the book is not without flaws, the pages delightfully come alive with every story. For example, in 'Friday, Saturday' (a story of two brothers seeking fortune, fame and the princess's hand in marriage), we arrive at the wedding night:

> [Then] out from below the bed comes this big broon hare.
> 'I'm gonnae get this broon hare,' he says. He's doon the stair an oot on his horse eftir this broon hare an it's goin roon aboot him in circles an he couldnae blaw saut on this hare's tail. He's eftir this hare on this clear moonlight night an he's ower fences an ower dykes an ower ditches. The hare would go a wee bit before him, then it wad stop an he wad come up on it an it wad go away again, till it led him away miles an miles fae the big hoose intae the moorland…

Willie MacPhee perfects the art of 'audio-description', but readers should not underestimate Sheila Douglas's role in carefully transcribing every word he speaks. Were I to choose one story demonstrating the storyteller's prowess, it must be 'Johnnie Pay Me for my Story'. This is a story within a story, with gloriously imaginative motifs woven through a complex sequence of events, that teaches us subtle lessons in life. This astonishing test of concentration and memory demonstrates the art of the old tinsmith who, at the age of ninety, could hold an audience in the palm of his hand.

Sheila Douglas is at her best when commenting on the stories, identifying essential qualities that kept them alive, distilling the wisdom they contain and summarising their relevance to everyday life. A list of Cant words is included, as are several pipe tunes, favourite songs and two songs composed by the author. This book is as much a labour of love as a tribute to a remarkable tradition bearer.

Margaret Bennett

Queen Amang the Heather: The Life of Belle Stewart
Sheila Stewart. Birlinn. ISBN 9781841585284. £7.99

Queen Amang the Heather is, on one level, an affectionate biography of the legendary matriarch of the Stewarts of Blair, by her immensely talented daughter. It is also a study of the travelling people of Scotland and, to a lesser extent, Ireland, focused on the Stewart family. Framed within Belle Stewart's lifetime (1906–97), this is an account of a life spent within a rich cultural environment, and amongst prodigiously talented people.

Born Belle MacGregor in a bow tent at Caputh, near Blairgowrie, Belle Stewart learnt her first song, 'The Twa Brothers', aged six. She married Alex Stewart and lived and worked in Scotland and Ireland. She performed widely in Scotland, England, Europe and North America with her musical family, including her husband, daughters Cathie and Sheila and, latterly, Sheila's children. Belle is presented as extremely hard working, optimistic in the face of adversity, generous of spirit and proud of her heritage. Possessed of a terrific sense of fun, she could administer a firm put-down. Performing at Sidmouth, for instance, the Stewarts met some new-age travellers: 'My mother… said to them… "Have you ever seen other travellers with matted hair, like yours, and no washin themselves?" "Well no," he said…, "maybe we will start a trend among your travellers"… "Not on your nelly," my mother replied.'

Stewart depicts the lifestyle and worldview of travellers in all their complexity. There is a great deal of information about traveller experiences, from berry picking to pearl fishing to hawking. This was, and is, a culture of great tenderness, nurturing creativity and valuing traditions, with a vibrant linguistic range including Cant and Scots. However, this is no whitewash; Stewart is honest about the deeply rooted prejudices travellers face; equally, she shows traveller society as – like the wider Scottish society that surrounds it – subject to problems, from alcohol abuse to domestic violence.

Stewart is revealing, too, on the nature of folk revival. While she is appreciative of the opportunities this gave the Stewarts and performers like Jeannie Robertson (Alex Stewart's cousin), she is alert to its inequalities: 'we never got one penny for singing our hearts out, not even from Hamish [Henderson]. Lots of them [collectors] thought we were only travelling people, and that they could do what they liked with us for nothing.' She is illuminating on the Stewarts' performance practices, too: 'We all had our own songs and we weren't allowed to dip into each other's. That's the way it was; my mother was the boss of what we could sing on stage.'

Perhaps unsurprisingly in a writer who is a wonderful interpreter of ballads, Stewart's own narrative is direct and understated, with emotion that is below the surface but no less expressive for that. Here, what the folklorist would itemise as *märchen* or legends, ballads or lyrics, become part of a continuous narrative. Recollections blend into anecdotes and are interspersed with tales, songs and music: supernatural tales like 'The Black Dog of the Stewarts' and 'The Headless Man'; Alex Stewart's pipe tune 'Iain Mhor' and Jim Reid's 'The Stewarts of Blair'. Pre-eminently, there are Belle Stewart's songs, including, of course, her famous composition 'The Berry Fields of Blair', along with tales, such as 'Aippley and Orangey'. The book also includes evocative photographs and moving tributes from family, friends and colleagues, many of whom are distinguished performers or scholars of song.

Queen Amang the Heather should be set alongside other insider accounts of travellers' lives: Betsy Whyte's *The Yellow on the Broom* (1979) and *Red Rowans and Wild Honey* (1990), Duncan Williamson's *The Horsieman* (1994) and those within Timothy Neat's *The Summer Walkers* (1996). Equally, it should be read beside Ewan MacColl's study of the Stewarts, *Till Doomsday in the Afternoon* (1986), with a soundtrack of *The Stewarts of Blair* (1994), Belle Stewart's *The Queen Among the Heather* (1998), Sheila Stewart's *From the Heart of the Tradition* (2000), MacColl's radio ballad *The Travelling People* (1969) and Martyn Bennett's reworking of Sheila Stewart's performance of MacColl's 'Moving on Song' on *Grit* (2003). Taken together, these provide a convincing record of the significance of the Stewarts within traveller, and national, expressive culture.

Stewart is highly conscious of changes in travellers' lives over Belle's lifetime: 'not only is berry time over, but also the Dundee fortnight, and the Glasgow and Fife fairs as well. The worst part of all for us travellers is no more ceilidhs round the outside fire and no more… keeping up our culture.' Belle Stewart, however, her contribution to music recognised by a BEM, was not downhearted and, in that spirit, she should have the last word: 'Noo, I hae been to balls and I hae been to halls/I've been in London and Balquhidder/But the bonniest lass that ever I did see/She was herding yowes amang the heather.'

Valentina Bold

The Enlightenment and the Book: Scottish Authors and Their Publishers in Eighteenth-Century Britain, Ireland, and America
Richard B. Sher. University of Chicago Press. ISBN 9780226752525. $40.00

Richard B. Sher's *The Enlightenment and the Book* is among the most penetrating and sustained analyses of the role of publishing in the Scottish Enlightenment, uniting new archival research with well and lesser known scholarship. Considering the interactions between authors, printers, publishers, booksellers and markets, Sher convincingly argues that the Scottish Enlightenment was as much a convergence of diverse material circumstances as it was of individuals and texts. He shows, for example, how the publishing agreements between Edinburgh and London publishers increased as a result of improvements in transportation, and led to an expansion in trade which generated the large sums that encouraged many Scottish thinkers to pursue publication. Many of Sher's insights are based upon a painstakingly compiled bibliography of Scottish Enlightenment books, which notes the publisher of the first British, Irish and American editions, as well as the price and number of editions a book went through. While such details may seem a bit dry at first, they allow for novel observations. For example, Irish booksellers and publishers in Dublin – which often pirated Enlightenment texts in the absence of a binding copyright law – lowered the price for books in Britain, Ireland, and America. In short, Irish book pirates helped to make the Scottish Enlightenment affordable and consequently extended its reach and influence to an international readership. As Sher observes, 'Dublin was the hinge on which the Atlantic dissemination of Enlightenment books turned.'

Sher also devotes a large portion of the book to resourceful Scots who moved to London, like Andrew Millar who became 'the greatest bookseller and publisher of the mid-eighteenth century', publishing key Enlightenment thinkers like William Robertson and David Hume. By the unusually young age of twenty-three, Millar had set himself up as a bookseller and publisher and one can understand the common temptation to view him as a self-made man who literally invented his own success. But as Sher argues, this easy explanation overlooks the importance of Millar's origins: 'Millar's career as a London bookseller and publisher can only be explained by understanding his Scottish background.' For example, by using his eight-year apprenticeship with the leading Edinburgh publisher James M'Euen as a starting point, Millar was able to take over M'Euen's bookshop in the Strand and begin publishing a set of titles that were based on M'Euen's own.

Sher's book also brings together the human, biographical details that are often missing in many publishing accounts, such as the agonising financial uncertainty that James Boswell underwent when self-publishing the *Life of Samuel Johnson* in 1791. Drifting into a state of 'timidity and indecision' as a result of an unexpected increase in publication costs which threatened the whole project, Boswell was faced with financial ruin. But, ultimately, he was determined to continue: 'I am quite resolved now to keep the property of my *Magnum Opus* and I flatter myself that I shall not repent of it.' In the end of course, Boswell was right to do so and, from the first edition alone, he made a sizable profit of £1,500, or around £140,000 in today's money.

One of the most useful aspects of the book is the long introduction which provides a much needed overview of the state of Enlightenment scholarship. The introduction – which you can read online at http://www.press.uchicago.edu/Misc/Chicago/752526.html – describes a fragmented field divided into various camps pursuing particular aspects of Enlightenment history. Sher warns that 'breaking up the Enlightenment into a multitude of unrelated segments exaggerates differences among geographical areas at the expense of their underlying similarities', and you can see his point. No doubt this is one of the reasons that the book is titled *The Enlightenment and the Book* and not *The Scottish Enlightenment and the Book*. However, it can be argued that Sher himself is contributing to the break-up of the Enlightenment by excluding the contributions of French, German and even American Enlightenment writers and publishers from his narrative. Of course you can hardly expect Sher to add to a monograph that already runs to nearly 800 pages, but he sets the book up for this critique and I suspect that it might have been Chicago University Press that opted for the expansive title rather than Sher himself. Another glaring excision is the lack of consideration of Enlightenment readers. Sher argues that a focus on historical readers has gone too far already and undermines the overriding significance of authors and publishers, but an overview on how Enlightenment texts were read would have been a valuable addition. However, against the background of Sher's achievement these are relatively minor critiques and the book is recommended reading for both scholars and general readers. At eight hundred pages it won't be read on the beach or the bus, but it should be read by anyone with an interest in the Scottish Enlightenment.

Ross Alloway

The Scottish World: A Journey into the Scottish Diaspora
Billy Kay. Mainstream. ISBN 9781845960216. £16.99

Emigration from Scotland has been a significant element in the country's history and there is a long-established Scottish diaspora in most corners of the world. Although many expatriates retained their identity and often celebrated aspects of Scottish culture, links to the home country were, of necessity, limited before the age of the internet and cheap international air travel.

These relatively recent developments have had two effects. First, they have allowed expatriate Scots to travel back to Scotland on a frequent basis. Second, they have stimulated interest in the Scottish diaspora within Scotland. Two examples are the increasing significance of Tartan Day, in the USA and Canada, as a focus for expatriates to express their national identity; and the launch of the Scottish Executive's Fresh Talent initiative, aimed in part at engaging with the diaspora and encouraging reverse migration and investment in the Scottish homeland. Billy Kay's book, with its widespread coverage of Scots abroad, has therefore appeared at a particularly appropriate time.

Billy Kay will be familiar to many for his writing and his broadcasts on various aspects of Scottish history and identity. Some, like his oral history series *Odyssey* in the early 1980s, were highly influential. He has travelled widely, often in search of material for his programmes, sometimes for pleasure as in his trips with the Tartan Army during World Cup campaigns, and he is also able to recall early school trips to foreign parts. These experiences have given him an extensive network of links and an almost unrivalled knowledge of the Scottish diaspora and have helped to inform this book.

Kay's approach to expatriate Scots is a sympathetic one and he believes that 'you can be a Scot even if you have not lived in Scotland for generations and, crucially, that your contribution to the Scottish debate is a valid one.' He writes of the generally positive way in which Scots are viewed abroad and, in particular, of the impact of a Scottish accent and the kilt in helping to make friends. Historically, this positive attitude towards Scots was a result of the strong educational tradition which meant that Scots who travelled abroad were literate and knowledgeable.

Indeed, the Scottish tradition of education and the early development of libraries helped to fuel the Scottish Enlightenment. Kay refers to the role of Scots in founding the *Encyclopaedia Britannica*, first published in 1768 in Edinburgh, and also the *Edinburgh Review* in 1802, which became a powerful force in British culture and political life and which circulated around the globe.

Individuals with Scottish ancestry have contributed significantly to their countries of adoption. Kay refers to Edvard Grieg, the Norwegian composer; David Buick from Arbroath, who helped develop the American automobile industry; and John Muir from Dunbar, the father of National Parks. Scottish music and literature have had important influences in North America, with Cape Breton in Canada still a place where Scottish traditional music has a home. Not all the influences were benign, however, and Scots settlers were also associated with the white supremacist movement in the southern United States and with the Ku Klux Klan. Mark Twain blamed Sir Walter Scott's novels for encouraging the South to embrace unreal historical romance rather than economic and social progress.

Kay's book is an impressive blend of history and present-day experiences, illustrated by extensive literary references and personal reminiscences. A chapter on the Auld Alliance is enlivened by both a discussion of cross-national influences on Scottish and French poetry and personal memories of filming a programme for the Edinburgh Festival, intriguingly entitled *Knee Deep in Claret*. Kay makes a number of pleas for more Scottish history to be taught in schools, and draws attention to the wealth of historical material often lying underused in local museums throughout Scotland. By using local artefacts and by demonstrating connections to far-flung places, history can, he argues, be made both exciting and relevant for young people.

What emerges most strongly from this book is a real sense of both nationalism and internationalism. There is a pride demonstrated across many parts of the world in a Scottish national identity and in Scottish history and culture. At the same time, it is clear that Scotland and the Scots have played a significant role in international trade, finance and development, and Scottish entrepreneurs have been outgoing and internationalist in their approach. This ability to be both national and international gives the lie to those who claim that nationalism is, by its nature, inward-looking and parochial. The Scottish world, argues Kay, literally knows no bounds. He delights in pointing out that the first man to set foot on the moon was a descendant of Liddesdale reivers, who carried with him on the Apollo 11 mission a swatch of Armstrong tartan.

Duncan Sim

Tugs in the Fog: Selected Poems
Joan Margarit. Translated by Anna Crowe. Bloodaxe. ISBN 9781852247515.
£9.95

Born in 1938, Joan Margarit is a Catalan architect who applies the same exactness of craft to his work in architecture as he does to his work in poetry, the foundations of which begin as precise and calculated structures, from which he builds upwards. His poems are orchestrations of everday events, observations, reflections on his own life, and for Margarit it is important to 'remain faithful to what we have felt at any given time' in those 'little moments of life' that permeate his work.

Time, memory and death are major themes in Margarit's poetry: 'Time that is inside us like the sand of a river, which little by little changes the shape of the coast.' Time is what changes us all and will ultimately annihilate everything; but before then, time houses memories, time is what on sea-journeys to Tenerife first brought Margarit to poetry, and it is the effects of time that may devastate but do not destroy him – when looking out at the sea at Cadiz he meditates on the inescapable fact of the death of his daughter Joana.

As if closer to prose-writing, the language of Margarit's poetry is direct and simple, and is characterised by a concision and exactness. The beauty of his work comes from its simplicity, but also from its rawness and harshness, especially when he is writing about loss. A master craftsman, Margarit is also an architect of the emotions.

The use of memory as a poetic vehicle, particularly in the poems from his 1999 collection *Estació de França*, achieves almost magical effects. The reader is taken on journeys through a universe of the senses and across time and space. And so it is not strange that in these poems his trains from *Estació de França* can arrive anywhere, or that the last lines of these poems can take us to unexpected destinations, too.

The poet's childhood in post-civil war Spain is a place his poems often come back to: 'the shadows of the war, within me, come from childhood's great fear'. Born into a Catalan family, his language was banned under the dictatorship, and his first poems were written in Castilian. Having worked now for many years in Catalan, he is regarded as the foremost poet in that language. Margarit's work is the embodiment of linguistic diversity; he now constructs his poems in Catalan and Castilian at one and the same time.

In her accomplished translations, Anna Crowe recreates the sonorous intensity of the originals, and brings Margarit's work to new readers, who surely will enjoy his trains.

Turo Delgado

The Edinburgh History of Scottish Literature
Edinburgh University Press

Volume 1 *From Columba to the Union (until 1701)*. Period Editors: Thomas Owen Clancy (to 1314) and Murray Pittock (1314–1707). General Editor: Ian Brown. Co-editor: Susan Manning. ISBN 9780748616152. £65
Volume 2 *Enlightenment, Britain and Empire (1707–1918)*. Period Editor: Susan Manning. General Editor: Ian Brown. Co-editors: Thomas Owen Clancy and Murray Pittock. ISBN 9780748624812. £65
Volume 3 *Modern Transformations: New Identities (from 1918)*. Period and General Editor: Ian Brown. Co-editors: Thomas Owen Clancy, Susan Manning and Murray Pittock. ISBN 9780748624829. £65

It was not so many years ago that one Scottish literary critic wrote of his disappointment with fellow critics for their 'refusal to engage with international developments in literary theory', and warned of the dangers for 'those involved in the culture of a small country… to fail to raise its eyes to the horizon and to wish to look only towards home-grown interpretative models'. This warning was made with some justification – at that time, the nature of Scottish literary criticism was generally inward-looking, and coupled with this was Scotland's 'continued anxiety about its political status', with that tendency of any small nation 'whose culture is under pressure to… cling tightly to traditional notions of itself, to emphasise purity and continuity, as opposed to plurality and change'.

Since that time there has, of course, been a huge transformation in this country – politically, economically, socially and culturally. Within the academic arena, there is full engagement with critical and literary theory, and as a serious subject of study within university literature departments, Scottish literature is now properly established. In response to the same critic's wish to see Scotland 'open to the wider worlds of cultural theory', it must be said that the *Edinburgh History of Scottish Literature* is 'theoretically orientated', and brings to these new assessments of Scottish literary production a range of critical methodologies and adopts a variety of analytical approaches – though not to the extent of alienating or excluding the general reader. Thankfully, the 'F' and 'B' words – Foucault and Bakhtin – are used but sparingly, and appear in only one chapter.

Once most commonly understood to refer to 'imaginative writing' or 'literary texts' in Scots or (created by Scottish writers) in English, the term 'Scottish literature' now must more accurately include the wide varieties of literary production in Gaelic, Welsh, Norse, Latin as well as Old French that have contributed to this country's diverse literary heritage. Coming almost twenty years after the publication of the four-volume AberdeenUniversity Press *History of Scottish Literature* – 'an important and pioneering work' to which the Edinburgh editors pay tribute – the *Edinburgh History* aims to be 'the most extensive, the most various and the most inclusive history of Scottish literature available to date'. And to a great extent this publication achieves these aims.

As the editors with no understatement acknowledge, each of the volumes is 'in itself of some substance'. By no means unscholarly, the *History* is highly accessible and straightforwardly readable; as such it bridges the gap between 'the specialised world of learned books' and 'the needs of a wider reading public'. With no detectable false modesty, the editors write that the *History* aspires to 'reliability and the intellectual rigour that comes from commanding knowledge gracefully worn'. These aspirations can be said to be realised in part.

Dispensing with the 'grand narrative sweep' and 'authoritative interpretations' of literary history of the past, the *Edinburgh History* offers a series of new perspectives, with an emphasis on a plurality of approaches: 'multiple authors, many stories, many forms, themes, approaches and angles of understanding.' And 'inclusivity' is very much 'a theme, both of intellectual discourse and architectonic structure', of the *History*. Though never purporting to be a cultural history of Scotland, this publication does consider the wider cultural context in which literature operates, and discusses at length other aspects of cultural production – that is, not simply literary works which belong to the domain of 'imaginative' writing, but oral literature, screen media, theatre and society, song, law writing, letters, journals and domestic writing, newspaper fiction and literary journalism as well as philosophical texts. With reference to the 'multiple contexts' in which the literatures of Scotland have been created – 'theological, historical, geographic, linguistic, philosophical and architectural' – each volume contains introductory chapters that describe the wider cultural context to the period it covers. The first volume devotes several chapters to the beginnings of Scotland and the creation of a historically (and politically) defined country, and the multiple linguistic roots in which the literary tradition developed. In the second volume, there are individual chapters on 'Scottish Literature: Criticism and the Canon', 'The International Reception and Literary Impact of Scottish Literature', 'Scotland's Literature of Empire and Emigration, 1707–1918' and, for the same period, a chapter on 'The Scottish Book Trade at Home and Abroad'. And in the third volume, there is a particular focus on the growing international significance of Scottish writing and the internationalising of Scottish literary scholarship in the past thirty years, particularly in continental Europe and North America. These important contextualising chapters are very much an identifying feature of the *History*.

Any literary survey of this kind will meet with criticism, not only for what it does, but also for what it doesn't do, and particularly for which writers it has chosen to exclude or has simply omitted. And for some there will be a temptation to put this work down too readily for its perceived weaknesses and for its editorial or ideological peculiarities. But it is just as important – if not more so – to acknowledge the strengths of a literary survey such as this, especially in its endeavours to reconsider and re-evaluate certain writers who have fallen out of fashion or favour. Tobias Smollett, after a long period of 'academic neglect and public indifference', is one of those writers being rehabilitated to that class of 'authors of the first distinction', (which rehabilitation has been assisted at least in part by the University of Georgia Press, which has embarked on the publication of a scholarly edition of Smollett's major works). And Byron too poses some interesting questions: 'half a Scot by birth, and bred/A whole one.' Though it was P.H. Scott who, elsewhere, mischievously described him as 'England's Scottish poet!', Alan Rawes in his chapter on his lordship argues, 'if Byron is a European poet, he is *also* an English poet; if he is an English poet, he is *also* a Scottish one.' A more troubling writer for critics to 'place' is J.M. Barrie. R.D.S. Jack writes, 'Barrie is a critical conundrum. The development of Scottish literature as a discipline may have raised the profile of most Scottish authors. Yet Barrie remains a major exception to that rule.' Jack's essay provides a radical assessment of Barrie's work.

With its emphasis on inclusivity, cultural diversity, hybridity and multiplicity, and its consideration of Scottish literature as 'a continuous and multilayered phenomenon', there is in the third volume, *Modern Transformations: New Identities*, surprisingly little discussion of modern popular fiction or popular writers; and none at all of Scottish Catholic writers, other than Spark; while the contribution of Jewish writers to twentieth-century literary production in Scotland is taken care of in one sentence. Whatever its shortcomings and omissions, the *Edinburgh History of Scottish Literature* does represent a hugely monumental contribution to Scottish literary studies and is bound to help shape discussion about this country's literature in this new century.

Michael Lister

Notes on Contributors

Eleanor Burnhill was born in London, grew up in Edinburgh and now lives in Dublin, where she works as a freelance journalist. She studied history at the University of Manchester before moving to Ireland on a bit of a whim. There she did a Masters in Journalism at Dublin City University. She recently went on a round-the-world trip but ended up in Dublin again. She works as a court reporter for Ireland International News Agency, reads the news for Today FM and occasionally writes for the *Irish Mirror* and other national newspapers.

Ron Butlin has an international reputation as a prize-winning novelist. Before taking up writing full-time he was, at various times, a lyricist with a pop band, a barnacle scraper on Thames barges, a footman attending embassies and country houses, and a male model. His works include the novels *The Sound of My Voice*, *Night Visits* and most recently *Belonging*; two collections of stories, *Vivaldi and the Number 3* and *The Tilting Room*; as well as six books of poetry. Besides his radio plays, much of his work has been broadcast in Britain and abroad. His fiction and poetry have been translated into over ten languages. Ticking the Boxes' is from *No More Angels*, to be published by Serpent's Tail in August 2007

Mike Faulkner was born in Northern Ireland but has spent most of his adult life in Scotland, initially working as a solicitor in Edinburgh and subsequently setting up the UK's first company to design, manufacture and retail Santa Fe style furniture. Following the collapse of the business in 2001, and the loss of a much-loved family home in Kinross-shire, he moved with his wife and two terriers to a wooden cabin on the otherwise uninhabited island of Islandmore on Strangford Lough, Northern Ireland. *The Blue Cabin* (Blackstaff Press, 2006), www.thebluecabin.com, is his account of island life.

Leontia Flynn was born in 1974 in County Down. She studied English Literature at Queen's University Belfast and competed a Masters at Edinburgh University. Her first collection, *These Days*, was published by Cape in 2004, won the Forward prize for best first collection and was shortlisted for the Whitbread Prize. She was named one of the *Guardian*'s 20 'Next Generation' poets in the same year. She is currently a research fellow at the Seamus Heaney Centre for Poetry at Queen's and is completing a second collection as well as re-working her PhD thesis on the poetry of Medbh McGuckian.

John Gilbert shared a flat with Stewart and Kate Parker in the 1970s in Belfast. During this time John contributed to an arts magazine called *Interest* and took a number of photographs of communities in Sandy Row and Divis. John made a living taking photographs and restoring a house at the same time that Stewart was working on his first play, *Spokesong*. He also worked with the Sandy Row Redevelopment Association and became involved with other communities through working at the Northern Ireland Housing Execuive. The experiences of seeing people's housing conditions at first hand led to John's interest in housing and he now has his own architectural practice in Glasgow, having left Belfast in 1976.

Alan Gillis is from Belfast. He studied and/or worked at Trinity College Dublin, Queen's University, Belfast and the University of Ulster, before moving to Edinburgh last year. His first poetry collection, *Somebody Somewhere*, was published by The Gallery Press in 2004. A new collection, which he hopes will be called *Hawks and Doves*, is currently in his publisher's hands. As a critic, he is the author of *Irish Poetry of the 1930s* (Oxford University Press, 2005), while his long-awaited meditation on King Kong has been published recently in the literary journal, *The Yellow Nib*.

Eamonn Hughes is a senior lecturer in the School of English and assistant director of the Institute of Irish Studies at Queen's University, Belfast. He specialises in Irish Literary and Cultural Studies, on which he has published widely. He has particular interests in autobiography and ideas of place. He edited *Northern Ireland: Culture and Politics 1960–1990* (Open University Press, 1991), and co-edited, with Fran Brearton, *Last Before America: Irish and American Writing* (Blackstaff Press, 2001) and, with Edna Longley and Des O'Rawe, *Ireland (Ulster) Scotland: Concepts, Contexts, Comparisons – Proceedings of ISAI 2002* (Cló Ollscoil na Banríona, 2003).

Fred Johnston was born in Belfast in 1952, educated there and in Toronto, Canada. He was co-founder of the Irish Writers' Co-operative in the Seventies, founder of the annual Galway-based Cúirt Festival of Literature in 1986. He runs the Western Writers' Centre (www.twwc.ie) in Galway. He received a Hennessy Literary Award for prose in 1972. Since then, he has published eight volumes of poetry, a collection of stories and three novels, most recently *The Neon Rose*. A collection of poetry, *The Oracle Room*, will be published by Cinnamon, UK, in the autumn.

Kapka Kassabova was born and raised in Bulgaria and educated at a French lycée in Sofia, a sixth form college in Essex, and two New Zealand universities. Since 1992 she had been based in New Zealand, but three years ago she moved to Britain. Her first collection, *All Roads Lead to the Sea*, won the 1998 NZ Montana Book Award for best first poetry book. Her novel *Reconnaissance* (Penguin NZ) won the 2000 Commonwealth Writers' Prize for best first novel in Asia-Pacific; her second novel was *Love in the Land of Midas* (Penguin NZ). She was twice the recipient of the NZ Cathay Pacific Travel Writer of the Year award, and her latest travel guide is the *Globetrotter's Guide to Bulgaria* (2007). Her first UK book was *Someone Else's Life* (Bloodaxe, 2003) and her new poetry collection, *Geography for the Lost*, will be published in 2007.

Nick Laird was born in 1975 in Country Tyrone. He attended Cookstown High School and Cambridge University, and later spent a year at Harvard as a visiting fellow. For several years he worked as a litigator and arbitration lawyer in London and Warsaw. In 2005 he published a poetry collection, *To A Fault* (Faber), and a novel, *Utterly Monkey* (Fourth Estate). He has received many awards for his fiction and poetry, including the Rooney Prize for Irish Literature, the Ireland Chair of Poetry Prize, the Jerwood Aldeburgh Award and the Betty Trask Prize. A new collection, *On Purpose*, will be published in August 2007 and a novel, *Glover's Mistake*, will be published in spring 2008. He lives in Rome.

Brian McAvera is a playwright, art critic and curator. *Picasso's Women*, *Yo! Picasso!*, and *Kings of the Road* are all published by Oberon Books, London. *Picasso's Women* has now been translated into nine languages. He has also written seven volumes of art history and criticism.

Alastair McCook lives in Portrush, County Antrim. He grew up close to the market town of Ballycastle on the North Antrim coast, where the annual Auld Lammas Fair remains the big day out on the local calendar. McCook has photographed the event for over twenty-five years and the human tableau of street traders, horse dealers and drunken bar room balladeers features prominently in his extensive archive. An exhibition of this work, *Praise the Summer Gone*, toured Ireland in 1994 and again in 2004. He is the author of three books on motor cycle racing: The *Power and the Glory: The History of the North West 200* (Appletree Press, 2001); *Days of Thunder: The History of the Ulster Grand Prix* (Gill & Macmillan, 2004); and *White Line Fever: A Photographic Celebration of Irish Road Racing* (Gill & Macmillan, 2006).

Medbh McGuckian was born and lives in Belfast where currently she is teaching creative poetry writing at the Seamus Heaney Centre, Queen's University. Her last two collections of poetry, *The Book of the Angel* and *The Currach Requires no Harbours*, were both from Gallery Press County Meath. She has four children. Her work is considered obscure and feminist but it is rather Irish and quasispiritual. She had read in many fastivals and at many universities throughout Europe and America. Her poems have been much translated and anthologised. Presently she is shortlisted for the Poetry Now Prize in Dublin.

Matthew McGuire was born in Befast and currently teaches Scottish and Irish literature at the University of Glasgow. His main area of interest lies in the late twentieth century, particularly the culture of late capitalism, including reconfigurations of class and the impact on the politics of literary representation. He has previously published work on Northern Irish fiction and the use of language in the fiction of James Kelman and Roddy Doyle. He is also the author of *The Essential Guide to*

Contemporary Scottish Literature, forthcoming from Palgrave MacMillan.

Bernard MacLaverty has published five collections of short stories and four novels: *Secrets & Other Stories* (Blackstaff Press, 1977); *Lamb* (Cape /Blackstaff Press, 1980); *A Time to Dance & Other Stories* (Cape /Blackstaff Press 1982); *Cal* (Cape /Blackstaff Press, 1983); *The Great Profundo & Other Stories* (Cape /Blackstaff Press, 1987); *Walking the Dog & Other Stories* (Cape /Blackstaff Press, 1994); *Grace Notes* (Cape /Blackstaff Press, 1997); *The Anatomy School* (Cape/Blackstaff Press, 2001); *Matters of Life & Death & Other Stories* (Cape, 2006). He has also written versions of his fiction for other media – radio plays, television plays, screenplays. Recently he wrote and directed a short film, *Bye-Child*.

Deirdre Madden is from County Antrim. Her novels include *The Birds of the Innocent Wood*, *Nothing is Black* and *One by One in the Darkness*. Her most recent novel is *Authenticity* and she is currently writing *Molly Fox's Birthday*. She lives in Dublin, where she teaches in Trinity College.

Sinéad Morrissey was born on 24 April 1972 in Portadown, County Armagh. She has published three collections of poetry: *There Was Fire in Vancouver* (1996), *Between Here and There* (2002) and *The State of the Prisons* (2005). She was the 2002 Poetry International Writer in Residence at the Royal Festival Hall and currently teaches Creative Writing at Queen's University, Belfast. Having lived and worked in Japan and New Zealand, she now lives in Northern Ireland. She was selected by the British Council to take part in the Writers' Train Project in China in 2003.

Frank Ormsby was born in 1947, in Enniskillen, County Fermanagh, and was educated at Queen's University, Belfast. He is head of English at the Royal Belfast Academical Institution. His books of poetry include the collections *Ripe for Company* (1971), *A Store of Candles* (1977) and *A Northern Spring* (1986). His most recent work is *The Ghost Train*, published in 1995. He was editor of the *Honest Ulsterman* 1969–89 and has edited the *Poetry Ireland Review* (numbers 53–56). Most recently he has edited *The Hip Flask: Short Poems from Ireland* (2001), a collection of Irish lyric poems including work by W.B. Yeats, J.M. Synge and Seamus Heaney, and *The Blackbird's Nest* (2006), an anthology of poems from Queen's University, Belfast.

Glenn Patterson has published several novels: *Burning Your Own, Fat Lad, Black Night at Big Thunder Mountain, The International, Number 5* and *That Which Was*. *Lapsed Protestant*, a collection of non-fiction, was published in 2006. He lives in Belfast, where he teaches on the MA in creative writing at Queen's University. A new novel, *The Third Party*, will be published in autumn 2007.

Tom Paulin was born in Leeds, Yorkshire in 1949 and was raised in Belfast. He was educated at Hull University and Lincoln College, Oxford. He is now G.M. Young Lecturer in English at Hertford College, Oxford. He is a well-known broadcaster and a regular member of the panel for the BBC television arts programme *Newsnight Review*. His collections include *A State of Justice* (1977), winner of a Somerset Maugham Award; *The Strange Museum* (1980), which won the Geoffrey Faber Memorial Prize; *Liberty Tree* (1983), and the acclaimed *Fivemiletown* (1987), which explores Northern Irish Protestant culture and identities. Later collections include *Walking a Line* (1994) and *The Wind Dog* (1999), which was shortlisted for the T.S. Eliot Prize. *The Invasion Handbook* (2002) is the first instalment of an epic poem about the Second World War. His latest collection is *The Road to Inver: Translations, Versions and Imitations 1975–2003* (2004), which brings together work from four decades. He lives in Oxford with his wife and two sons.

Andrea Rea began working as 'Troubles Archivist' for the Arts Council of Northern Ireland in June 2006. Before that she had worked in the Theatre Archive of the Linen Hall Library on the archive of John Boyd, writer, BBC producer and literary advisor to the Lyric Theatre, Belfast. Andrea also writes articles and classical music reviews for Belfast's *Newsletter*, the oldest continually-published English-language newspaper, and is a freelance writer and broadcaster for BBC Radio Ulster.

Marilynn Richtarik is an associate professor of English at Georgia State University in Atlanta, Georgia. She is the author of *Acting Between the Lines: The Field Day Theatre Company and Irish Cultural Politics, 1980–84*, published by Oxford University Press in 1995. She is currently working on a critical biography of Stewart Parker.

Dawn Wood works as a lecturer at University of Abertay Dundee. She is currently writing a PhD on the science and art of animal husbandry. She is also a painter and exhibits in Dundee and Aberdeen. Her poems have been published in *TLS*, *Poetry Review*, *PN Review* and *Magma*. Dawn is workshops manager for StAnza, the poetry festival at St Andrews.

Howard Wright lectures in art history at the University of Ulster, Belfast. He has published poetry in the *TLS*, *The Shop* (Cork) and *Magma*. Blackstaff Press, Belfast, will publish his first collection, *King of Country*, later this year.